Behavioral Tax Research: Prospects and Judgment Calls

EDITED BY JON S. DAVIS

American Taxation Association, Sarasota, Florida

American Accounting Association
5717 Bessie Drive
Sarasota, FL 34233

Library of Congress Catalog Card Number 95-83074

ISBN 0-86539-076-2

Printed in the United States of America
10   9   8   7   6   5   4   3   2   1

Behavioral Tax Research

CONTENTS

FOREWARD

This is the third tax research monograph published by the American Taxation Association (ATA). Its scope was proposed by Robert Halperin, Chair of the 1993-94 ATA Research Resources and Methodologies Committee, and Jon Davis, a committee member. A number of experienced behavioral researchers have contributed to this monograph, which was edited by Jon Davis. The first three chapters detail researchers' experiences with moving a particular research idea and paper forward into an accepted article. The three remaining chapters provide a perspective on behavioral tax research and suggestions for the future.

As with the first two monographs, the ATA is grateful to the KPMG Peat Marwick Foundation for its generous financial support of this project.

ANNA C. FOWLER
President, 1993-94

PREFACE

The 1993–1994 Research Methodologies Committee, chaired by Robert Halperin, was charged to produce a research monograph on behavioral tax research. This volume is the result of that charge. Since the scope of the monograph was too great to complete in one year, the work was continued by the 1994–1995 Research Methodologies Committee. It is the third research monograph published by the American Taxation Association.

The monograph is organized in two parts, each with a distinct goal. In Part I, three accounts of the research process are provided, detailing the development of published behavioral research papers, from the inception of a research idea through data collection and ending with the review process and ultimate publication of the research results. Throughout, the authors note judgment calls that they made, difficulties encountered, and recommendations to others given their experiences in the research process. This part of the monograph aims to support doctoral students and new faculty in their research quest.

The three authors for Part I were selected to provide diversity in viewpoints. Linda Johnson reports on her experiences as a new faculty member, focusing on her dissertation work and the issues surrounding conversion of her dissertation into a publishable research report. Charles Swenson addresses the unique issues encountered while performing an experimental economics study. Finally, Michael Schadewald describes a cognitive study developed as part of a research program examining analogical reasoning in tax professionals, emphasizing difficulties encountered in the review process.

The second part of the monograph critically evaluates past behavioral tax research with the aim of identifying prospects for future work. As in Part I, diverse views are presented. Edmund Outslay provides a past editor's outlook on the future of behavioral tax research. K. Dianne Jackson, Michael Shields, and Ira Solomon bring an outside perspective to the table. Shields and Solomon have worked primarily in other areas of behavioral accounting and Jackson is a doctoral student in tax. Finally, Michael Roberts and Chris Purdie introduce a practitioner view on the usefulness of behavioral tax research.

Thanks go to the KPMG Peat Marwick Foundation for agreeing to fund the publication of the monograph and its distribution to the members of the American Taxation Association. The contributors to the monograph are also gratefully acknowledged for the generous contribution of time and effort that made this volume possible.

CONTRIBUTORS

Jon S. Davis
Associate Professor of Accountancy
and Weldon Powell Fellow
University of Illinois at Urbana–
Champaign

K. Dianne Jackson
Doctoral student in Accounting
University of Memphis

Linda M. Johnson
Associate Professor of Accountancy
Northern Illinois University

Edmund Outslay
Professor of Accounting and Past
Editor of *Journal of the American
Taxation Association*
Michigan State University

Christine Purdie
Educational Consultant
Price Waterhouse LLP, New York

Michael L. Roberts
Associate Professor of Accountancy
University of Alabama

Michael S. Schadewald
Associate Professor of Accounting
University of Wisconsin at
Milwaukee

Michael D. Shields
Arthur Andersen Professor of
Accounting
University of Memphis

Ira Solomon
KPMG Peat Marwick Distinguished
Professor of Accountancy
University of Illinois at Urbana–
Champaign

Charles W. Swenson
Professor of Accounting
University of Southern California

Part I

JUDGMENT CALLS

1

THE STORY BEHIND PREPARERS' EVALUATIONS OF JUDICIAL EVIDENCE

Linda M. Johnson

This chapter provides an account of the process that culminated in an article on preparers' evaluations of judicial evidence that appeared in the Spring 1993 issue of *The Journal of the American Taxation Association (JATA)*. This chapter is a personal history; it focuses on the problems and issues I encountered while working on my doctoral dissertation. Consequently, while some issues doctoral students may face when working on a dissertation are discussed, no attempt is made to address every judgment or problem that may be encountered when conducting behavioral tax research or completing a dissertation.

I begin by describing my search for a dissertation topic. I then describe the decisions I made when designing the study and the issues I considered when constructing and pilot testing the instrument. Subsequently, I discuss my experience with identifying and locating appropriate subjects. Finally, I discuss the process of turning my dissertation into a publishable product, including how I targeted my working paper and how I responded to the reviewers' comments.

SELECTING A TOPIC

Before enrolling in the doctoral program at Arizona State University, I worked for three years in the tax department of what was then Arthur Young & Co. Based on my work experience, I knew when I started the doctoral program that I was interested in teaching and doing research in the tax area. Although my interest in tax shaped my course of study, I was well into coursework before I developed an interest in behavioral research. I had read about the research being done on tax compliance in a doctoral tax seminar, including what seemed to be an increasing number of papers focusing on the role of tax preparers in the compliance process. Because the research on preparers was relatively new, I chose to focus on this area as I neared the completion of my coursework and began thinking about a dissertation.

After studying all the tax preparer research I could find (both published and unpublished), I began to think seriously about a topic. For me, formulating a suitable research idea was the most difficult part of the research process. Throughout my doctoral coursework my natural tendency was to take a theory I learned in a psychology seminar or a current working paper in auditing and attempt to apply it in a tax setting. Although this approach was useful for the proposals I wrote in my doctoral courses, it was less helpful in my attempt to find a dissertation topic.

It was clear from discussions with my committee that a dissertation was significantly broader in scope than the proposals I had prepared for my coursework, which were primarily replications or straight-forward extensions of existing studies. More importantly, I realized that once the dissertation process began, it would be at least two years before I could submit a working paper for publication. I was concerned that, if my research idea originated from a recently published article or a well-circulated working paper, other researchers might be working on a similar projects. I had visions of an article similar to my research appearing in print before I could submit a working paper from my dissertation. Furthermore, I was afraid that, even if other researchers were not working on exactly the same idea, the incremental contribution of my research might be limited once other papers on the topic were published. Finding a dissertation topic that would make a contribution to the tax literature three years down the road was more difficult than I had expected.

One afternoon, while another doctoral student and I were waiting at an airport after attending a conference, I mentioned my difficulty in identifying a suitable research topic for my dissertation. Being unfamiliar with what tax preparers do, he asked me to explain the (legal) research process. I diagramed the research process on a cocktail napkin, starting with the identification of the issue and the fact situation, followed by the search for authoritative evidence. I explained that preparers often locate authoritative evidence by using annotated tax services, like Commerce Clearing House's *Standard Federal Tax Reports*. However, except for the Code and regulations, these services only summarize the various sources of authority. Preparers interested in reading the full text of specific rulings and cases must consult other sources.

He then asked how preparers select which rulings and cases to pursue. After describing the difference between reasonable basis and substantial authority, I explained that until recently, a reasonable basis was sufficient to recommend an aggressive position. Therefore, the strategy was to locate sources of authority that provided support for the client's desired outcome. However, since the enactment of the substantial authority provisions, preparers could no longer attend only to pro-taxpayer evidence, but instead must objectively consider all evidence before rendering advice to a client. When asked whether I believed that preparers objectively attended to all authoritative evidence, I responded that I was uncertain, but that it was plausible that they didn't. After all, the client, not the government, was paying for the advice. It was during that conversation that I realized I had taken the wrong approach to finding a topic. Instead of looking for a popular or "hot" theory to apply in a tax setting, I should have started by drawing upon my practice-based experiences to identify issues facing professionals and worried about finding an appropriate theory later.

Once I decided to examine whether preparers objectively evaluate evidence when conducting research, I began to consider which theories could explain why preparers might attend more to pro-taxpayer evidence than to pro-IRS evidence. Prior empirical research had shown that preparers act as client advocates, which was consistent with my personal experiences from working in public accounting. Results from studies conducted in psychology found that individuals exhibit a confirmation bias by understating the importance of opposing evidence and overstating the significance of supporting evidence. Based on these findings, I thought I could make a reasonable case for why preparers acting as client advocates might unintentionally understate the relative importance of opposing authoritative evidence, and potentially recommend a position for which substantial authority did not exist. At this point, I was beginning to clarify some of my research questions. Did preparers use confirmatory processes when evaluating authoritative evidence? Was the use of confirmatory processes related to client advocacy? Did the use of confirmatory processes result in biased recommendations? With a rough idea of the research questions in mind, I began to consider the experimental design.

ISSUES ENCOUNTERED WHEN DESIGNING THE STUDY

Most studies in psychology that examined individuals' use of confirmatory processes involved subjects with differing initial beliefs about a particular topic. After reviewing the same set of mixed (opposing and supporting) evidence, subjects' revised beliefs were measured. An examination of the directional change in subjects' beliefs enabled researchers to determine which type of evidence was more influential in shaping subjects' revised beliefs.

The typical experimental design used in psychology studies was similar to that used by Lord et al. (1979). Lord et al. purposely recruited students with differing initial beliefs about capital punishment's deterrent efficacy. Subjects were provided with the same evidence, some that confirmed capital punishment's deterrent efficacy, and some that did not. Due to subjects' differing initial beliefs, half the subjects perceived the evidence confirming capital punishment's deterrent efficacy as supportive evidence, whereas the other half perceived it as opposing evidence.

Although I liked the idea of measuring preparers' beliefs before and after being provided with mixed authoritative evidence, I did not believe that this particular design was appropriate for a tax setting. Specifically, I felt it would be difficult to find enough preparers whose initial beliefs about an ambiguous tax issue were contrary to their client's position. I believed that in an ambiguous area of the tax law, a considerable majority of preparers would have similar (pro-client) initial beliefs. Therefore, to test whether preparers use confirmatory processes, I modified the traditional experimental design and altered the authoritative evidence so that one group of preparers would perceive the evidence as supportive (pro-taxpayer), while the other group would perceive it as opposing evidence (pro-IRS). My first thought was to try to accomplish this by altering the outcome of the judicial evidence.

In objectively determining the relevance of judicial authority, preparers' judgments (normatively) should be based on the facts of the case, not on the outcome. Preparers should not judge a court case as more similar to a client's situation because the court ruled in favor of the taxpayer or as more dissimilar because the court ruled in favor of the IRS. If preparers' judgments about the relevance of the case are affected by the outcome, it would provide evidence that preparers use confirmatory processes. Once I had some idea of how I was going to test for preparers' use of confirmatory processes, I was ready to design an instrument that would require preparers to judge the relevance of judicial evidence. However, before designing the instrument, I first considered who would be completing it. In particular, I thought that a shorter task might be necessary if the subjects were practicing tax professionals, whereas a longer task might be possible if the subjects were students.

Since I was attempting to gain insight on how tax practitioners make decisions when faced with ambiguous areas of the tax law, I felt the most appropriate subjects would be professional tax preparers with experience conducting research. To ensure availability of a sufficient number of subjects (80 to 100), I felt it was necessary to limit the time required to complete the task to under one hour.

ISSUES FACED WHEN CONSTRUCTING THE INSTRUMENT

I wanted the task to mirror the actual research process used by preparers; however, I realized there was a trade-off between task length and task realism. Eventually, I decided to sacrifice some task realism in exchange for the opportunity to use practicing tax professionals as subjects. Establishing a balance between the length and realism of the task required careful planning of each aspect of the instrument.

Selecting a Research Issue

I established two primary criteria for selecting the research issue. First, since the purpose of the study was to examine preparers' evaluations of judicial evidence on issues involving ambiguous areas of the tax law, the issue should require preparers to examine sources of authority beyond the Code and regulations. Second, given the time constraints, I felt that the research issue needed to be one for which the applicable Code and regulations provisions were short, which would allow the subjects more time to evaluate the judicial evidence.

Because it had been several years since I had worked in public accounting, I looked to my committee for guidance in finding a research issue that met these criteria. Two members of my dissertation committee, Mike O'Dell and Jim Boyd, taught Masters of Tax courses and were familiar with recent developments in the tax area. I found their input to be invaluable not only in selecting a client issue, but also in summarizing the authoritative evidence. (A third committee member, Hal Reneau, was invaluable in helping me with design issues).

After exploring a number of possible issues to use in the instrument, I presented my top choices to the committee. My committee then provided their thoughts about the appropriateness of each issue. My first choice was ruled out because within the past five years, the Ninth Circuit had ruled on a case similar to the proposed client issue. My committee was concerned that some subjects, especially those working in the Ninth Circuit, might recall this case and use it (either in addition to or instead of the four cases provided in the instrument) when completing the task. We finally agreed that of the various issues I had presented, the reasonableness of compensation paid to a sole shareholder of a corporation appeared to best meet my criteria. Not only could the

Code and regulations provisions addressing this issue (IRC §162(a)(1) and Treas. Reg. §1.162-7(a) and (b)) be reproduced on one page, but they also provide limited insight as to what constitutes reasonable compensation. This would require subjects to concentrate on the judicial evidence in making a recommendation. In addition, I decided to include a question in the instrument asking subjects if they had previously conducted research on reasonable compensation. The responses to this question allowed me to identify the responses of subjects who may have previously researched this issue for a client. (Twelve percent of the subjects who participated in the study had previously conducted research on reasonable compensation.)

Selecting the Number of Cases to Include in the Instrument

To manipulate the court's decision between two groups, it was necessary to use an even number of cases so that subjects would evaluate the same number of pro-taxpayer and pro-IRS cases. I felt that limiting the task to two cases might reduce the realism of the task. Although including six cases might be more realistic, in an effort to minimize the length of the task, I decided to include four cases.

For reasons described in footnote 10 of the article, the four cases needed to be of equal judicial weight to all subjects; therefore, the cases needed to be either four Tax Court or four Claims Court cases. To test whether preparers evaluate judicial evidence differently depending on the outcome of the case, I also needed four cases that were equally convincing when presented as either pro-taxpayer or pro-IRS. Although summarizing actual court cases might have resulted in a more realistic task, I could not find four actual cases that met my criteria. Therefore, I decided to construct the four experimental cases.

Selecting the Information to Include in Each Case

I used actual court cases as guides to construct the four experimental cases in order to maintain a high degree of task realism. I began by reviewing numerous court cases on reasonable compensation and listing the various factors the courts used in rendering their decisions. After identifying eight frequently cited factors, I constructed four cases so that the facts of each case contained four factors that supported the taxpayer's claim as to the reasonableness of the compensation and four factors that supported the IRS's position. The four factors chosen to support the IRS's and taxpayer's positions were different in each case.

To keep the task manageable, I decided that each case should be no more than one page in length. I wanted the information in the case to resemble what preparers see in practice. Since preparers who use

annotated tax services to initiate their research are aware of the outcome of the case prior to reading it, I placed the court's holding at the
top of the page. The rest of the case closely followed the organization
of actual court cases, with the facts of the case presented first, followed
by the positions of the IRS and taxpayer. In actual court cases, the opinion also includes a summary of the court's reasoning. Although manipulating the court's holding was relatively easy, manipulating the
court's reasoning (to concur with the court's holding) was more difficult to accomplish without unintentionally introducing a bias into the
design. If I wanted to infer that observed differences between the
groups were caused by knowledge of the court's decision prior to reading the case, it was necessary that the court's holding be the only difference between the two versions of the case. Accordingly, I decided
not to include the court's reasoning, thereby sacrificing some realism to
improve the validity of the results.

Deciding Whether to Include a Planning or Compliance Issue

Once the four cases were completed, I constructed the hypothetical client situation using the same eight factors. Because I did not want any
one court case to more closely resemble the client's situation than
another case, it was important that each case was similar to the client's
fact situation in some ways, but different in others. A problem that
continued to bother me when constructing the client situation was
whether to present it as a planning or compliance issue. I wanted to
avoid including both types of issues in the design, since it would double the required number of subjects. Unfortunately, I was not sure
which type of issue would produce stronger evidence of confirmatory
processes if preparers did in fact use such processes. If I selected one
type of issue and found no effect, I would wonder whether the other
type of issue would have produced a significant result. Ultimately, I
had little choice but to include planning versus compliance as a variable in the study.

I manipulated this variable between subjects at the time they were
presented with the client's research issue. Subjects who received the
compliance issue were asked whether the president's compensation of
$296,000 would be reasonable in light of the client's fact situation. Sub-
jects who received the planning issue were informed that currently the
president's compensation was $200,000, but that the Vice President of
Finance was considering paying the president a bonus equalling 30%
of gross sales in excess of $1,500,000. Using current estimates, the
bonus would add $96,000 to the president's compensation. Subjects
then were asked whether the president's compensation would be
deemed reasonable.

Measuring Advocacy

In my dissertation, I hypothesized that the advocacy role caused preparers to use confirmatory processes when evaluating authoritative evidence. Manipulating the court's decision between two groups of subjects and asking them to rate the relevance of each case enabled me to test for preparers' use of confirmatory processes; however, I still needed a method for measuring subjects' advocacy.

After scanning the accounting, legal, and psychology literatures, I could not locate a questionnaire that measured degree of advocacy. This left me with two options: (1) construct my own measure, or (2) delete the part of the study that required an advocacy measure. Because this aspect of the research process had not been explored previously and because I believed that the advocacy role influenced preparers' evaluations of authoritative evidence, I was hesitant to leave it out of the study. I began studying various methods of scale construction by reading books on the subject. I chose to use Likert's (1932) scaling technique because prior studies consistently found it to be reliable and effective.

In developing an advocacy scale, I thought about various scenarios which might depict preparers acting or not acting as client advocates. I started by constructing 36 statements that described the behavior of a tax preparer in a variety of situations. Two such statements are provided below.

> After reviewing judicial authority in an area where the Code and regulations are ambiguous, if I am unsure as to whether the position would be judicially supported, I *would recommend* taking the position.

> In an area where the Code and regulations are ambiguous, no judicial authority exists and the only other source of authority is a revenue ruling which does not support taking the position, I *would not recommend* taking the position.

I attempted to word half the statements in a way that would cause preparers acting as client advocates to agree (e.g. with the first statement). The remaining statements were worded in a way that would cause preparers who did not act as client advocates to agree with the statement (e.g. with the second statement). I then asked six practitioners for feedback on each statement as to whether they believed a preparer acting as a client advocate would agree with that statement. Only statements about which there was unanimous agreement among the six practitioners were retained. Accordingly, seven statements were dropped from the advocacy scale.

Next, I asked a several practicing tax professionals to respond to the remaining 29 statements. Responses to each statement were correlated with the preparer's total score. Twelve of the 29 statements were not statistically significant, leading to elimination from the final scale. This left me with seventeen statements for the advocacy measure.

Pilot Testing the Instrument

When using archival data, mistakes in the design generally can be corrected and the data rerun with relatively little additional cost. In behavioral research, a flaw in either the design or the instrument often can be the difference between a publishable paper and rejection. Since my study would require approximately 100 experienced tax preparers as subjects and the instrument would take a minimum of 30 minutes to complete, I realized I probably would have only one opportunity to run the experiment. This made it especially important that any "bugs" in the design or instrument be worked out in advance. As a result, I conducted fairly extensive pilot testing of the instrument.

I wanted the pilot subjects to be similar to those that would participate in the final experiment. In my quest to locate enough subjects for the pilot, I discovered I needed to be more flexible about when subjects could complete the task. Firms appeared more willing to provide subjects after June 15th. Also, more subjects were available if I allowed them to complete the task at their convenience. Personnel at the participating firms agreed to administer the experiment and mail the responses back to me. In a cover letter to the participants, I emphasized the importance of not discussing the task with others and not using sources other than those provided in the packet. Since the primary purpose of pilot testing was to identify potential problems with the instrument, I was willing to give up total control of the experiment in exchange for feedback from a greater number of subjects.

During the initial pilot test, I elicited written feedback on the realism of the task, the information contained in the instrument (what was missing, what was unnecessary), and the problems encountered when completing the task. For the most part, subjects felt the task was realistic, especially since seniors and managers often review the summarized findings of a staff person's research. Regarding the completeness of the instrument, one subject did suggest including the court's reasoning with the judicial authority. However, for reasons previously mentioned, this information could not be incorporated into the instrument.

The feedback received was useful in identifying potential problems. For example, through pilot testing, I found that subjects were confused over my wording of the question asking them to assess the probability the position would be judicially supported. In the initial instrument, the question read,

Suppose a deduction for the full $296,000 of the president's compensation is taken on the return and is later challenged by the IRS. Without examining any further administrative or judicial evidence, what do you feel is the probability that the position would be supported by the courts?

Feedback from the first pilot test indicated there was some confusion over the term "the position." Did it mean the position they ultimately recommend, the IRS's position, or the position to take the deduction? I corrected this problem before the second pilot test by replacing "the position" with "the deduction for $296,000." This apparently cleared up any confusion as no comments were made regarding this particular question in subsequent pilots. After three pilot tests, I no longer received substantive comments; therefore, I felt the instrument was ready for the final experiment.

OBTAINING SUBJECTS

Since my research issue focused on whether preparers evaluate evidence using confirmatory processes, the most appropriate subjects for this experiment were tax professionals with experience conducting tax research. Accordingly, I did not consider using undergraduate students or graduate tax students with no public accounting tax experience for this experiment. For purposes of internal validity, I needed assurances that subjects would use only the information contained in the instrument to complete the task. I also needed to be sure that subjects completed the task independently. Since these restrictions essentially required that I be present during the experiment, I eliminated the possibility of administering the study through a mail survey and decided that the most efficient way to collect the data would be to administer the experiment during a firm's training sessions.

When I began my search for subjects, I was aware of one firm's policy of allowing audit researchers to conduct behavioral experiments during the first Friday morning of their two-week audit training sessions. I was not aware, however, of any firm having a similar program for behavioral tax research. I was fortunate that I was ready to administer my experiment in July, since most firms begin their tax training sessions in the late summer or early fall. When I contacted a firm about subjects, I explained the nature of my study, the task, the time required for administration (feedback from the third pilot test indicated that the task took approximately 30 minutes to complete), and that I was primarily interested in administering the instrument at firm training sessions.

The first firm I contacted explained to me that their training sessions would not allow for a 30-minute experiment. I was told that 10 minutes was the most they could offer. The second firm I contacted offered to distribute the instrument to employees who volunteered to complete it "after hours." They too were concerned about the length of the study and thought it was unlikely that 100 employees would volunteer to complete a 30-minute survey on their own time. At this point I was left with the following options: (1) continue asking firms for tax personnel to complete a 30-minute task, (2) consider using another method to collect the data, or (3) reduce the length of the task.

Since I did not believe I could accomplish my research goals with a 10-minute task, I considered the third option to be a last resort. As for the second option, I considered using graduate students with public accounting experience or administering the instrument somewhere other than at firm training sessions, but neither alternative seemed ideal. Although part-time Masters of Tax students with practical experience would have been suitable subjects, Arizona State's program was not large enough to provide me with enough subjects for my study. Finding enough subjects would involve contacting other schools with Masters of Tax programs and making arrangements to administer the study. Although gathering the data by visiting individual firm offices was also a possibility, it would have resulted in a lengthy data collection process. Accordingly, I decided to continue my search for a firm that would allow me subject time.

I was fortunate to find such a firm; however, there were three conditions. First, I was responsible for my own transportation to the training facilities. This did not present a problem for me, since I had intended to pay for my expenses. Second, I was to contact the instructors, explain my research to them, and ask for permission to administer the study during their sessions. Third, I had to agree to distribute an exit survey prepared by the firm. The purpose of the survey was to determine whether participants felt it was worthwhile to take time away from firm training sessions to participate in these types of research experiments. (Subjects responded on an 11-point scale ranging from absolutely not (−5) to absolutely yes (+5). Although opinions varied, the mean response to this question was 1.5). Once I located subjects to complete the instrument, the data collection process went smoothly, as did the rest of the dissertation.

THE PUBLICATION PROCESS

The three questions I faced when I started to convert my dissertation into a working paper were: (1) Where should I submit the article or articles? (2) How many articles should I extract from my dissertation? and (3) How should I convert a 100 page dissertation into a 20 page working paper?

Targeting the Journal(s)

Over the years, I had noticed that, with a few very notable exceptions, much of the significant behavioral tax research was published in *JATA*. With this in mind, I chose *JATA* as a target journal for my dissertation research. Other doctoral students (both tax and non-tax) questioned my decision to submit my paper to *JATA* instead of to *The Accounting Review*. However, at the time I was ready to submit a working paper, I heard that *The Accounting Review* was interested in publishing tax papers with broader accounting implications. Since I did not believe that my article had significant implications for accountants in general, I chose to submit my paper to *JATA*. I also felt that *JATA* readers would be more interested in my research findings.

One or Two Papers?

The data yielded several interesting findings. First, the results indicated preparers' recommendations on an issue involving an ambiguous area of tax law were biased. Second, the data suggested that the bias resulted from preparers' use of confirmatory processes. Third, it appeared that the bias was related to client advocacy. Given these findings, I was confronted with the issue of whether to incorporate them into one working paper, or to split them up into two papers (e.g., the first two findings in one paper, and the third in another).

By reporting all of my results in one working paper, my chance for publication in *JATA* would be maximized. On the other hand, the possibility of two publications from my dissertation was tempting. In determining which avenue to pursue, I considered the risks involved if I chose to submit two working papers. For me, the worst case scenario would be to submit two working papers and discover through the review process that one of the papers did not make a strong enough contribution to warrant publication. I decided that the probability of publishing one paper reporting on all my research findings in a top journal like *JATA* was better than the probability of publishing a paper reporting on only part of my research findings.

Turning the Dissertation into a Working Paper

Once I had decided to focus on one working paper, I needed to condense 100 pages into 20 pages. I had noticed that articles appearing in *JATA* and other journals were not organized like my dissertation. Consequently, a four page summary of each chapter would not have resulted in a well-written, cohesive article. Since I did not want my working paper to read like a condensed version of my dissertation, I essentially wrote the paper from scratch, working from an outline that stated what I intended to accomplish in the paper. I found Zimmerman's (1989) article on improving a manuscript helpful in this regard.

Once I completed the first draft of my working paper, I distributed it to my dissertation committee for their feedback. After I had the opportunity to incorporate their comments, I sent the second draft of the manuscript to colleagues I had met through the doctoral program, conferences, and interviews. Although this process took several months, the comments I received were helpful, which might have been the difference between a favorable first review and an outright rejection.

Responding to Reviewers' Comments

The article that appeared in *JATA* is significantly different from the working paper I originally submitted from my dissertation. This is primarily due to the incorporation of the comments and suggestions from the reviewers and the editor. For example, the original manuscript contained three hypotheses; the revised manuscript contained six. In addition, Figure 1 was added to the revised manuscript to illustrate the relations among the variables.

In the sections below, I discuss some of the issues raised during the review process. I also discuss how I attempted to resolve these issues. I was fortunate that the reviewers not only raised issues, but also provided guidance for resolving them. I was also fortunate that the editor, Ed Outslay, was very thorough in taking the comments from both reviewers and emphasizing which comments were important to address. Although I am aware of instances where authors have received conflicting comments and were required to use their judgment to resolve them, there were no such conflicts in my experience.

Are preparers client advocates? In my paper, I contend that preparers acting as client advocates should perceive judicial authority that ruled in favor of the taxpayer as supportive evidence and judicial authority that ruled in favor of the IRS as opposing evidence. One reviewer questioned whether in many instances,

> ...the preparer may initially believe that the client position will not be supportable. In such a context, confirmation bias (as it has been defined

in the literature) would predict that one would tend to overweight *opposing* (and NOT supporting) evidence since it is consistent with the initial belief. Hence, your predictions do not follow from the prior literature. The missing link is evidence demonstrating that, with increased advocacy, there is an increased tendency to form an initial belief in favor of the taxpayer.

The reviewer suggested that I examine the mean value for the variable PreProb (the subject's assessment of the probability of judicial success prior to reviewing the judicial evidence). He thought that, if the PreProb mean was small (≤ 50%), one would expect a confirmation bias to lead to an overweighting of *opposing* evidence. An analysis of the data showed the variable PreProb to be greater than 50%. Bifurcating the data, I found that subjects whose PreProb was ≤ 50%, like those whose PreProb was > 50%, used confirmatory processes to evaluate judicial evidence, but to a lesser extent. I responded to this issue by adding footnote 6 and H6 (which tested the relationship between Advocacy and PreProb) in the revised manuscript. Because of this reviewer's comment, H5 was later added in the revised manuscript to test the relationship between preparers' initial beliefs (PreProb) and their use of confirmatory processes.

What about the differences between the planning and compliance issues? As discussed earlier, type of issue was included as an independent variable. If the results showed that preparers exhibit confirmatory processes in both planning and compliance issues, then including both types of issues would enhance the generalizability of the results. The results, however, indicated a greater use of confirmatory processes among subjects receiving the planning issue. I suppose I could have included in the working paper only the data from subjects who received the planning issue; however, the results of both the planning and compliance issues were presented, even though I had no idea why the difference had occurred. During the review process, one reviewer suggested that I include a discussion in the paper providing some rationale for the observed difference.

In responding to this comment, I began by thinking about the different situations preparers encounter when faced with a planning versus a compliance issue. In planning issues, if the preparer's research does not fully support the client's position, the preparer has the opportunity to adjust the client's facts to coincide with the research findings. This opportunity, however, is not available with compliance issues. I hypothesized that it might be possible that, when preparers conclude from their research that the client's position does not have substantial authority, they may feel less responsibility in a compliance situation since the client failed to bring the issue to their attention before the transaction occurred. Therefore, preparers researching a planning issue might use more confirmatory processes (because they feel greater responsibility) than those researching a compliance issue. In response to the reviewer's comment, I included this discussion in the revised manuscript (first paragraph on page 13).

Relatedness versus relevance. Another issue raised during the review process was the wording of the question asking subjects for their relevance ratings for the four cases. In that question, I asked subjects which case they felt was most related to the research issue and asked them to assign it a rating of 100. One reviewer commented,

> What might a subject think when asked about how *related* a case is to the issue at hand? Your answer is that this measure defines how relevant the case is with regard to determining the probability that the issue would be decided in the taxpayer's favor by a court review. If I am an advocate for the client, I might believe that the supportive cases are the most related because it is the supportive cases that I will have to 'hang my hat on.' That is, the case may not be any more relevant to assigning a probability for taxpayer success but it is more *related* because the supportive cases are more critical. There may be 10 cases going against the client's position and one case for. This one supportive case may be the most related because it is the only hope for taking the client's position.

The reviewer asked me to think about whether my measure of "relatedness" was a measure of objective relevance or some sort of subjective relevance (i.e., relevant to making the argument for the client). Although it was not my intention, I had used the terms "relevance" and "relatedness" interchangeably throughout the question. To resolve this issue, the reviewer suggested I determine the "true relevance" of each court case using a separate group of subjects. This would require having the preparers evaluate the relevance of each case without knowledge of the court's holding. If these preparers find the four cases to be equally relevant to the issue, it would suggest that when subjects were informed of the court's holding, they responded that the supportive cases were more *related* to the research issue. I took the reviewer's advice and attempted to establish the true relevance of each case. I then included a discussion of my findings in the two paragraphs beginning with the last paragraph on page 18.

A similar issue was raised in regards to my measure of relevance. The comment was,

> Although a close reading of your case instructions indicates that the four cases could be scored equally if the subject so desired, I'm not sure the subjects responded in this manner. The task seems to demand a rank-

ing of the four cases. I understand your approach (i.e., to elicit relative ratings) but I'm not sure it was successful. Perhaps you could address this question by reporting the number of subjects who rated at least two cases equally. The more often this happened, the more likely it is that the subjects responded to this task in a manner other than a pure ranking approach. In short, if subjects felt forced to rank the four cases, your other results are suspect.

The reviewer suggested that I count the number of subjects that assigned equivalent ratings to at least two of the cases. My findings, which I report in footnote 21, suggest that subjects understood that they were asked to rate (not rank) the four cases.

Incorporating subjects' recommendations. The original manuscript submitted to *JATA* contained three hypotheses (H1, H2, and H4 from the article). One reviewer questioned why I had ignored the subject's recommendation decision, even though I had collected the data necessary to analyze it. The reviewer felt that the paper would be more informative if hypothesis tests were conducted on recommendations as well, especially given the work done in auditing that suggests it is important to look at actual recommendations when examining the effects of factors on professional judgment.

In response to this question, H3 was added to test the effects of assessing higher probabilities of judicial success on the *strength* of preparers' subsequent recommendations. In my comments to the reviewer, I provided the following example of when preparers' use of confirmatory processes *may* (but not always) cause them to make an "overly aggressive" recommendation to the client.

Assume two preparers, Preparer A and Preparer B, both believe that substantial authority exists if the probability of judicial success is at least 40 percent. Further assume that Preparer A objectively (i.e., without the use of confirmatory processes) determines that the likelihood that a position would be judicially supported is 35 percent. Preparer A would then conclude that substantial authority did not exist and therefore should recommend to the client either that the position not be taken on the return or that the position be disclosed on the return. Now assume that Preparer B researches the same issue and uses the exact same authorities as used by Preparer A, but that Preparer B uses confirmatory processes when evaluating the authorities. As a result of such processes, Preparer B determines that the likelihood of success is 45 percent, not 35 percent. Preparer B would then believe that a substantial authority exists and that the client would not need to disclose the position on the return to avoid the accuracy-related penalties.

Rather than provide this lengthy example in the revised manuscript, I added a paragraph (second paragraph on page 14 of the article) explaining that because subjects were not asked for their thresholds for substantial authority, I could not use the data from my study to determine whether the probabilities subjects provided exceeded their thresholds. (In hindsight I realize this would have been an appropriate question to ask). Consequently, I could only test whether the *strength* of their recommendations had been affected.

After responding to the specific comments and concerns of both reviewers and the editor, I resubmitted the manuscript and waited for a response. A few months later I received word that my article had been accepted, contingent on some editorial changes. I made the changes and within a few weeks received word that my article would appear in the Spring 1993 issue of *JATA*.

SOME FINAL THOUGHTS

From my observations, I concluded that much of behavioral tax research replicates research that has been done in other disciplines. This includes my research, which replicates in a tax setting the research performed in psychology on confirmatory processes. Rather than use an experimental design that had been successfully used in various psychology studies, I altered the design to create a more realistic task. Of course, the alteration could have resulted in problems with the internal validity of the study; however, my hope was that I could detect problems through extensive pilot testing.

When writing this chapter, I realized that many of the reviewers' comments were concerns over the wording used in the instrument. Through my dissertation defense and subsequent presentations of the study during the interview process, I had the opportunity to receive feedback on my theoretical development and experimental design *before* I ran the experiment. Unfortunately, I had not completed the instrument prior to defending my dissertation. Therefore, I missed out on the opportunity to receive feedback on it during the defense. I believe that if I had the opportunity to present the instrument along with the paper, some of the reviewers' concerns would have been raised before I ran the experiment.

In subsequent research projects, I have not been very conscientious about getting feedback from colleagues prior to administering experiments. In many instances, I later discover problems with the study that require additional data collection. Had I taken the time to have a few colleagues provide feedback on the instrument, it is possible that these mistakes would not have been made. When working with student subjects, rerunning the study may be of little consequence; however, I have found it becomes more of an issue when practitioners are used as subjects.

REFERENCES

Likert, R. 1932. A technique for the measurement of attitudes. *Archeological Psychology:* 140.

Lord, C., L. Ross, and M. Lepper. 1979. Biased assimilation and attitude polarization: The effect of prior theories on subsequently considered evidence. *Journal of Personality and Social Psychology* 37 (November): 2098–2109.

Zimmerman, J. 1989. Improving a manuscript's readability and likelihood of publication. *Issues in Accounting Education* 4 (Fall): 458–466.

2

THE ODYSSEY OF A PUBLISHED EXPERIMENTAL ECONOMICS STUDY

CHARLES W. SWENSON

This chapter chronicles an experimental market study (co-authored with Herman C. Quirmbach, Associate Professor of Economics, Iowa State University, and Cynthia C. Vines, Department of Accounting, University of Arizona) forthcoming in the *Journal of Public Economics*. The chapter discusses the successes and problems of this study with the intent of providing some perspective to young academics, or experienced ones who wish to publish in the area of experimental economics. While no article can serve as a map through the research project jungle, this one might at least help you locate some clear paths through the jungle.

OVERVIEW OF THE ARTICLE

The issue of who bears the burden of the corporate income tax has considerable theoretical and policy implications.[1] Despite the importance, econometric evidence on this issue is either conflicting or non-existent. Difficulties in using field data to test general equilibrium (GE) tax incidence is to be expected, since in the "real world" up to 40 years of data might be needed to measure long run factor mobility. In such a long time frame, a lot of confounding events can occur, making for difficult econometric analysis. We felt that the contribution of the Quirmbach,

---

1. For example, a policy consideration is corporate tax incidence, e.g., if the corporate tax is increased, some of it may be passed on to consumers.

Swenson, and Vines (1995) study was in providing the initial real empirical test of whether GE tax incidence theory could be upheld. The advantage of the experimental setting was that a tight, controlled test of theory could be performed in a setting where a "long-run" economic environment was possible.

The experimental subjects were student volunteers (from a variety of majors) at the University of Southern California who participated in one of six three-hour experiments. Average payment to these subjects was $65; the pay scale is discussed later in the chapter. Three of the experimental sessions were run without (sans) taxes, and three with corporate taxes. In each session, there were twelve participants: three sellers of capital who used their sales proceeds plus their shares of corporate and non-corporate profits to buy outputs; three labor sellers who used their sales revenue to buy outputs; three corporate producers who bought capital and labor to produce corporate output to be sold to consumers; and three non-corporate producers who also bought labor and capital to be sold to consumers. The decision to use three subjects in each side of every market is discussed later.

Each market period lasted eleven minutes, and there were ten such periods.[2] The experiments were run in a dedicated experimental economics laboratory using the MUDA (Plott 1993) software. Factor sellers/consumers were endowed with units of inventory and spendable cash, while producers were endowed only with decreasing returns to scale Cobb-Douglas production technology, which was preprogrammed into the MUDA system. In the with-taxes experiments, a 50% tax was imposed on the purchase price of capital, and the tax collections were redistributed equally to all consumers because of the general equilibrium setting.

The experiments found that the imposition of a tax on corporate capital resulted in the flow of capital into the non-corporate sector, and a decrease (increase) in the relative use of capital in the corporate (non-corporate) sector. The relative price of both corporate and non-corporate output fell. Output in the non-corporate (corporate) sector increased (decreased). All of the foregoing results were consistent with the theory. The policy implications were that the experiment demonstrated the distortive effects of a tax on corporate capital, and showed that in the long run, when capital was free to move between sectors, the tax was partially borne by the owners of capital.

2. Based on slightly less complicated multiple market experiments (Davis and Swenson 1993) which had eight minute periods, we estimated that eleven minute periods would be necessary. Figuring in subject paperwork, etc., between periods, this allowed for ten periods in a three hour experiment.

PRODUCTION

Let's face it. While we love what we do (okay, some days it's only a paycheck), performing research is much like producing and marketing a product. This part of the chapter discusses the production of the research paper in the following stages: idea, implementation, and analysis.

Idea

Reconstructing the genesis of this paper provides a confusing glimpse of the creative process. The concept seemed to have originated in a Ph.D. seminar in taxation which I taught at the University of Arizona in 1986. Jon Davis (then, a Ph.D. student in the class) and I batted around the idea of testing the impact of rapid tax depreciation on fixed asset acquisition in an experimental market. It later occurred to me that the general equilibrium incidence of corporate taxation could be tested the same way. In fact, there were a couple of nice chapters in the Atkinson and Stiglitz (1980) text on the topic, one of which we covered in the course. The idea resurfaced in 1989, when I supervised Cyndi Vines' dissertation on the incidence of corporate taxes on the insurance industry. She was a logical co-author choice, not only because of her theoretical background, but also because of her experimental economics and econometrics training.

The project was very exciting for two reasons: general equilibrium tax incidence had not been satisfactorily proven with econometric data, and no one had ever attempted a true general equilibrium experimental economics study. But three major issues lurked: funding; eventual marketing to an accounting journal; and the adequacy of our economics training.

"Mister, can you spare 100,000 dimes?"

A figure typically offered up as the cost of doing an experimental economics study is about $5,000. We estimated we'd need about double that amount. Since the KPMG Peat Marwick Foundation had been extraordinarily generous in the past, we thought they might be interested in funding another project. Although the Foundation had a reputation for funding purely academic work, we weren't above pointing out in our proposal that if GE tax incidence was demonstrated (not falsified) in our experiments, then corporate tax increases will probably end up being borne by just about everyone else. That is to say, such tax increases would largely miss their target.

Fortunately, the Foundation funded us. However, we underestimated the cost of subject fees because of false starts, subject training, and replications. This underfunding led me to conclude that when applying for subject fees, one must figure the highest amount that it will cost, and then add 30 to 40% to this amount (this is based on my experience over a number of projects). Also, one must cast a wide funding net; with downsized business school budgets, a patchwork of funding sources may be necessary.

Selling Freezers to Eskimos

Although our research can be a consumption good, our careers will be longer if we can also publish our projects. Our concern here was that general equilibrium tax incidence was probably an economics, and not an accounting, topic. Although I have refereed numerous papers in both economics and accounting journals, I still don't have a sense of what constitutes tax accounting research. My impression is that my colleagues are as confused as I am. Clearly, the greater the institutional richness, the more likely a reviewer will judge research to be related to accounting. Because of the vanilla nature of our corporate tax, our gut(less) reaction was to avoid disinterested editors and reviewers at accounting journals, and pursue an economics journal.

This judgment call can be made at various stages of a project. My suggestion is that it be made at the incipient stage to avoid a later train wreck. This is not to imply that a project should be bent, spindled or mutilated to increase its chance of publication in an accounting journal. But during the early stages of an accounting academic's career, reputation can be enhanced by publications in accounting journals.

Speak Softly and Carry a Smart Economist

The final problem was humbling: did we have the training (and horsepower) to do the analytic/theory work for the project? After all, no economist has actually done such a project before. Cyndi understood tax incidence theory quite well, and I had published an article on applying one particular form of GE model, input-output analysis. In a previous experimental market study, Jon Davis and I had solved for partial equilibrium tax incidence. But with four markets, no natural price levels, and recycling of profits and government expenditures into the economy, this experiment was going to be much more complex.

The prescription was Professor Herman Quirmbach, a Princeton-educated theoretical economist. He had previously expressed an interest to me in doing experimental work. When I contacted Herman about participating in this project, he agreed to work with us. As a consequence, the project's quality was greatly enhanced. Based on my experiences, I strongly encourage tax accounting researchers to enlist economists for their experimental studies. In addition to improving the study, we learned a great deal from our economist co-author.

Implementation

The personnel, resources, and strategy thus decided, the first stumbles of the great journey began. First, we needed a theoretical GE tax incidence model. Most rigorous public economics books had them, but they did not incorporate essential ingredients: upward sloping supply, and downward sloping demand curves, or their equivalents. Such curves are necessary to ensure profits for money-motivated human subjects in an experimental economy. Moreover, the production processes which were modeled in textbooks also ensured zero profits for producing firms.

So, we had to start from scratch. I blithely wrote out a system of equations for each of the four markets[3] and attempted to solve them much like the Davis and Swenson (1993) partial equilibrium model. After a week of messing with Lagrangians, I shipped it to Herman. He later flew out and rewrote everything, solving for competitive equilibrium prices and quantities in terms of endowments of capital and labor, and profits. At this point, it was still at a symbolic/continuous form level, so I needed to plug in some actual labor, capital, and profit levels which would meet three criteria: 1) they should be at most in the low double digits to reduce keystroking by subjects and to keep the number of trades at a workable level; 2) pre- and post-tax competitive equilibrium (CE) prices and quantities should be quite different (to give clear theoretical predictions); and 3) the CE prices and quantities should be close to (if not exactly) integer values, since the software we had allowed only integer prices and quantities.

After plugging in the symbolic equations into Mathematica and iteratively solving, I was—after an embarrassingly long time—able to arrive at some candidate values. A sanity check of these values by my co-authors, followed by some integer programming work in Excel, confirmed the original candidates. At the risk of being overly pedantic, the work here was necessary because it's not enough to predict "sorta" equilibrium and hope there is a qualitative difference in results across experimental manipulations. Indeed, the *sine qua non* of economics-based experimentation is point predictions, which allow for very fine tests of theory[4].

---

3. Labor, capital, corporate output, and non-corporate output.

4. We operationalized corporate taxes as being imposed on corporate capital (as opposed to profits), consistent with the literature on long-run tax incidence.

Enter Human Beings

Prior experimentation has shown that human beings rarely conform precisely to the predictions of economic theory, and we had no reason to expect subject behavior to be different here. So, only experienced subjects (i.e., who had previously been through unrelated double auction experiments) were used in order to devote more training time to experiment-specific issues, rather than spending time on the MUDA system, profit accounting, etc. The potential criticism of using only experienced subjects is that it might be claimed that we have a non-representative subject pool comprised only of subjects who like such experiments and who might have certain expectations. We felt that this was an acceptable trade-off because the enormous complexity of the experiment made it necessary. Fortunately, I was running a series of unrelated double-auction experiments for another project, and this group of people became feeders for the GE experiments.

Another human issue was the number of subjects to be used in each market. The USC School of Accounting/KPMG Peat Marwick Experimental Economics Lab has 17 workstations. Through past studies, I have learned that some redundancy is necessary[5], and a minimum here would be one extra computer for each type of subject in addition to one computer per subject. This technological constraint interacted with the human element as follows. Previous studies have shown that having two or fewer agents per market biases against competitive equilibrium (duopolies are non-competitive by nature), four agents are sufficient for competition, and there is limited evidence that three are sufficient to attain a CE. Thus, sixteen machines would be necessary, or one machine for each subject, plus one backup machine for each subject group. The pilot test would determine whether our subjects would act "as if" competitive in our three-person markets.

The training issue was non-trivial. We wanted to provide sufficient training so that subjects entered the experiment understanding everything except the manipulations (and how others react to them). But, we didn't want to suggest behavior, or allow them to collude or strategize. In walking this tightrope, we decided that because of the enormous complexities of their tasks, producers would be allowed to bring their instructions home after the training session, which they would bring back the next day when the experiment was held. Once we made the

---

5. Occasionally, hardware or operator error creeps in and renders a machine useless. Hardware error might include keyboard failure, screen failure, etc., which cannot usually be predicted. Operator error includes subjects accidentally rebooting the machine while the experiment is in progress, etc.

decision, we allowed all subjects to take home their instructions. Although we verbally instructed subjects not to collude, and we screened subjects for potential collusion (having roommates as participants), and a post-experimental questionnaire indicated no problems, there was always a chance of contamination and/or attempted collusion.

The training sessions themselves were a full three hours, with practice GE experiments of four periods, which used different parameters than those used in the actual experiments.

"The Best-Laid Plans of Mice and Men..."

With the theoretical and implementation issues seemingly solved, we were ready to float our trial balloon. If the pilot worked we were going to count it as a real experiment. One uncertainty was the number of proctors; in the training session, three were required to handle the large volume of questions. All three showed up for the first experiment, but only one was necessary (this occurred for the other five sessions as well).

The results of our pilot were unexpected. While actual quantities were very close to predicted CE's, prices got close to CE by the second period, but then started to inflate at an incredible rate. They were twice what they should have been by the final period, and the price trajectory was reminiscent of post-World War I Germany. Since there was no natural numeraire, any nominal prices were allowed so long as relative prices were as predicted. The pilot's relative prices turned out to be quite close to predictions. Since nothing was otherwise wrong with the experiment, we decided to run another one, and got very similar behavior.

The consistent inflationary behavior was pretty heady stuff; we thought we'd stumbled into something like "wishful thinking" across an entire microeconomy. Reality soon slapped us in the face: The third experiment featured deflation, the fourth flat prices, and the fifth and sixth very mild inflation. While relative prices were fairly close to predictions for all of these sessions, the differing price paths may end up on the television program Unsolved Mysteries.

The typical experimental problem of no-shows did not occur. We recruited 15 subjects for each 12-person experiment, but there was very little attrition, largely in part because of an incentive-aligning pay scheme. We paid them $20 for training, collectible at the end of the actual experiment. Extras were paid $30, which included a $10 appearance fee. On the "money matters" theme, I have found that $15 an hour is an appropriate pay rate, published (older) pay rates notwithstanding. The $15 rate is based on subject responses on exit questionnaires.

However, my subjects have been mostly USC undergraduates who may have higher monetary expectations than subjects in other parts of the country.

On Making the Data Confess

After we finished the experiments, we had to decide how to present a summary of the data. Although we decided to graph nominal prices, the actual prices used in data analysis were relative (to the actual prices of labor). Statistical tests faced the usual two problems: how to deal with data that are not independent, and how much of the data to analyze. The second problem is one of deciding when CE has been reached (i.e., most learning is completed). A fixed effects version of the regression test for this in Davis and Swenson (1993) revealed a constant, albeit small, equilibrium bias for all periods. So, we decided to use all periods. The non-independence problem in theory invalidates the use of statistical tests; in practice, econometricians who work with field data ignore this and control for it by the use of dummy variables, fixed and random effects models, etc., meanwhile fixing error autocorrelation with some generalized least squares (GLS) procedure.

We ended up taking the path of least resistance and reported simple mean prices and quantities by period, without any accompanying statistics. Thus, like most published experimental market studies, we resorted to "interocular" comparisons. A principle motivation for avoiding statistical analysis was the fear that the referees would be theoreticians and/or experimentalists who were not experienced econometricians, and would not understand the analysis. Fortunately, there were distinct qualitative differences in means between the two types of experiments in a direction predicted by theory. The exact point predictions were not achieved, but they were fairly close.

MARKETING

"If You Build a Better Mousetrap, They Will Beat a Path to Your Door."

At all costs we wanted to avoid the marketing faux pas of positioning the paper as simply a more sophisticated version of the venerable DA market experiment. Two "hooks" appeared obvious: no one had ever attempted to see if GE would work in an experimental microeconomy, and GE tax incidence appeared provable (falsifiable) in a laboratory where the truly "long run" could be noiselessly observed.

The initial drafts emphasized both. Presentations at the AAA annual convention, the ATA midyear convention, and in an economics class at the University of Arizona went well. Audiences thought the paper interesting, had few specific comments (this may have been due in part to the 30 plus equations), and agreed that it was an economics paper. The decision to submit to the *Journal of Public Economics* was based on my good experience there with a previous publication, when I received conscientious reviews and six-week turnaround. The "swift justice" aspect could not be overvalued because two of us were going up for promotion in the near future.

The Critics' Line Forms to the Left

Turnaround time was about seven weeks. One reviewer was generally favorable, but was quite concerned about the "seeding" of profits, wanting to know exactly how this occurred and whether it engineered the results. Because the MUDA system was not written to allow for the real-time calculation and distribution of firm profits to capital (firm) owners, we endowed them with profits (cash) at the beginning of each period equal to expected profits at the CE. This was fudging slightly on one part of the experiment, but there was no way around it. We offered this rationale, together with a better explanation of seeding, in the revision.

Reviewer 2 was considerably less charitable. I have noted that if you want three opposing views on a paper, get two referee reports. No exceptions here. He liked what we did, but was skeptical about the varying price level issue, low efficiencies, and differences across sessions. Efficiencies or the actual economy-wide profits as a percent of the theoretical maximum were about 85%, on average. To put this in perspective, single-market double auction experiments typically sport 95–100% efficiency levels. In other multiple market experiments (Davis and Swenson 1993; Goodfellow and Plott 1992) efficiencies dropped to 90–95%. So, given the complexity of our study, 85–90% was to be expected. This reasoning appeared in the original draft. No sale; the referee was skeptical. Reviewer 2's most serious criticism was that there was not enough data. He felt that more than two experiments per session were necessary to see if there was any consistency across experimental sessions. There was also the usual slew of minor editorial comments which added insult to injury.

The editor's letter invited a resubmission, but was non-committal. The letter stated that the journal would be willing to consider a revision, but that we should keep in mind that the journal was pressed for space. The last warning could also be a polite British way of telling us that the odds were against us. We decided to take no chances; we reduced the manuscript to two thirds of its original size. The removal of all discussion, graphing, and analysis of nominal prices did the job, but it was like gnawing off a limb. We thought that the nominal price analysis was the most interesting by-product of the experiment. The removal of the equilibration model discussion was another major page-saver. One thing I have learned in ten years of being on both sides of the revision process: authors need to comply *exactly* with editor's suggestions.

Will Work for Subject Fees

The biggest hurdle was obtaining funds for an additional two experimental sessions. Surprisingly, when we showed Michael Diamond (then the USC School of Accounting Dean) and Andy Bailey (then Accounting Department Head at Arizona) the letter from the editor, and explained that this was a top economics journal, they came up with $1,200 each. In times of financial stress at universities, this was a sign of good faith.

At this point, let me digress and discuss how we responded to reviewer suggestions. We made the decision to run additional experiments because we agreed with the reviewer. In any experimental session, some idiosyncratic behavior can occur, and usually three experimental sessions per treatment are necessary to have enough data that the idiosyncratic behavior averages out and is small relative to behavior resulting from the experimental treatments. We also complied with all of the referee's other suggestions, none of which we really disagreed with. My approach to dealing with referee comments is that, unless they are completely incorrect, you do your best to comply with them. To put it bluntly, it is worth swallowing a little pride if you can get the work published.[6]

Fortunately, the two experiments went smoothly. Efficiency was a bit higher than that of previous sessions, which combined with a revision of our original efficiency estimates, put aggregate (across all experiments) efficiency at 90%, which turned out to be enough to satisfy the reviewers. The second referee requested statistical tests for the revision; in fact, one additional reason for suggesting additional experiments was to have enough data to perform statistical tests. In the revision, we ran regression models with prices and quantities as dependent variables, with dummy variable regressors indicating a with-taxes experiment.

---

6. This strategy once backfired for me. For a study which was finally rejected on the third round, I dutifully complied with a hostile referee's suggestions except for one issue which could not be corrected. My subservience seemed only to breed further aggression and the reviewer argued convincingly to the editor for a rejection in the third round.

We opted for a continuous trend variable and full transformation GLS AR(1) adjustment to the standard errors. This model provided a better fit of the data than did other specifications, such as fixed effects models. Luckily, our significance tests of mean differences were significant with or without the adjustments. Cyndi is a good econometrician and the results were solid. But, we also presented raw mean data by period so the reader could see that the statistical results were not a fluke, and because (as noted previously) this where most experimental economists live.

Before resubmitting, Cyndi had some colleagues read the manuscript for clarity. Somehow, we were able to resist the temptation to submit before we were completely satisfied. All that remained was the correspondence. In our memos to the reviewers, we began with the standard statement of gratitude, and addressed each review comment point by point. Some observations here for newly–minted Ph.D.s: 1) addressing each issue flatters a referee, and 2) ignoring a comment either infuriates or arouses suspicion, both of which increase likelihood of rejection. If a comment cannot be satisfactorily addressed, it is far better to own up and throw yourself at the mercy of the referee than to use smoke and mirrors.

We closed the memos and the letter to the editor with a statement that we spent $2,400 on the additional experiments, thus enabling the referees to assuage their guilty consciences with an acceptance. We also pointed out to the editor that the Slim-fast version of the new manuscript would not add too many pages to the journal. Because of the quality of the journal, we had put a high priority on the revision and completed it in a couple of months. So it made sense to express mail it to the editor in London.

Closing the Deal

The editor's letter came back about eight weeks later with a conditional acceptance. A couple of references were necessary. We mailed back the revisions in a week.

SOME FINAL OBSERVATIONS

I'll Take Door Number One… and Door Number Two

This was a high risk project which fortunately paid off big. This is not always the case, and I encourage young authors to form a portfolio of high and low risk projects.

On Playing in Groups

My experience with co-authoring has been uniformly good, because of the high quality of academics I've worked with. Three things I've found to be true are: 1) things get done slower since there are invariably coordination and distance problems; 2) you spend less time than if you'd attempted the project yourself; and 3) the product is better than what you would have produced yourself. With the decrease in research funding, collaboration with academics at other institutions broadens the funding base, and appears to be a worthwhile strategy. Another benefit of coauthored projects is that group judgements are usually better than your own. Throughout this chapter, I have mentioned a number of instances when we made judgement calls[7]; all of the important ones were made jointly.

Westward, Ho!

There are still many unexplored topics which can be addressed by experimental economics. There are plenty of tax areas for which there is conflicting or weak field evidence, and there are a number of theories (pick up any issue of *Journal of Public Economics*, for example) that have never been tested. The growing acceptance of the method in economics and accounting journals makes the methodology all the more publishable.

    7. Sometimes these judgement calls were implicit, i.e., we didn't ponder them much. For example, in retrospect, we could have come up with at least a dozen journals which might have been suitable outlets for the study, but we instead went with a gut reaction.

REFERENCES

Atkinson, A., and J. Stiglitz. 1980. *Lectures on Public Economics*. New York: McGraw–Hill.

Davis, J., and C. Swenson. 1993. Experimental evidence on tax incentives and the demand for capital investments. *The Accounting Review* (July): 482–514.

Goodfellow, J., and C. Plott. 1990. An experimental examination of the simultaneous determination of input prices and output prices. *Southern Economic Journal* 56 (April): 969–983.

Plott, C. 1991. A computerized laboratory market system and research systems for the multiple double auction. Social Science Working Paper No. 783, California Institute of Technology, Pasadena.

Quirmbach, H., C. Swenson, and C. Vines. 1995. An experimental examination of corporate tax shifting and general equilibrium tax incidence. *Journal of Public Economics* (forthcoming).

3

BEHAVIORAL TAX RESEARCH REGARDING ANALOGICAL REASONING

MICHAEL S. SCHADEWALD

INTRODUCTION

This article describes my experience in conducting and publishing behavioral tax research regarding analogical reasoning. In particular, I will discuss "The Use of Analogy in Legal Argument: Problem Similarity, Precedent, and Expertise," which is a paper that I co-authored with Urton Anderson, Gary Marchant, and John Robinson. The paper was published in the June 1993 issue of *Organizational Behavior and Human Decision Processes.* I will describe why we wrote the paper, how we conducted the research, and how we resolved the problems that arose during the review and publication process.

The article is organized as follows. Section I discusses how this paper fits into a stream of research regarding the use of analogy in tax problem solving. Section II provides a synopsis of the paper, including the motivation for doing the study, the development of the hypotheses, the empirical work, and the conclusions we drew from the study. Sections III and IV focus on the story of how we published the paper. Section V discusses what I learned about behavioral tax research from this project.

OVERVIEW OF ANALOGY RESEARCH STREAM

Research Team and Objectives

The research team consisted of Urton Anderson, Gary Marchant, John Robinson, and me. Urton and Gary were primarily behavioral audit researchers, whereas John and I were tax researchers. Analogical reasoning was the topic of Gary's dissertation (Marchant 1989), and therefore Gary had unique expertise regarding the analogical reasoning literature in psychology.

From the start, we were interested in conducting a broad stream of research regarding the use of analogy in tax problem solving. Our initial research objectives were quite ambitious:

- Develop a theory of the cognitive processes involved in tax problem solving, with an emphasis on the role of analogical reasoning.

- Obtain empirical evidence regarding the use of analogy by tax professionals in applying decided court cases, including the conditions under which tax professionals are more likely to correctly or incorrectly apply case law.

- Investigate the role of expertise in the use of analogy by conducting experiments with both expert and novice tax professionals.

- Examine the effects of client advocacy on the use of analogy by tax professionals.

- Apply our model of tax problem solving to investigate the effectiveness of different instructional strategies on a student's ability to identify and resolve tax issues.

Our research drew heavily from psychological research regarding analogical reasoning. We were particularly influenced by Adams et al. (1988), Ashley (1988), Frensch and Sternberg (1989), Gentner (1983), Gick and Holyoak (1980; 1983), Holland et al. (1986), Holyoak and Thagard (1989), Lockhart et al. (1988), Novick (1988), and Sternberg (1977). There was little prior accounting research regarding the use of analogy, other than Marchant (1989), which investigated the role of analogical reasoning in auditors' generation of hypotheses.

Published Articles

This stream of research was conducted from 1988 through 1993, and involved a significant amount of empirical work. A total of 433 tax professionals and 612 graduate and undergraduate tax students participated in our experiments. The research resulted in the following four published papers regarding the use of analogy in tax problem solving:

- Marchant et al. (1989) presents a model of the cognitive processes underlying legal reasoning in both the tax compliance and tax planning settings.

- Marchant et al. (1991) reports the results of three experiments that compare the performance of novice and expert tax professionals in using analogy to apply decided court cases.

- Marchant et al. (1992) reports the results of an experiment that examines the effects of both analogous and disanalogous court cases on the tax problem solving performance of novice and expert tax professionals.

- Marchant et al. (1993), the subject of this article, reports the results of two experiments that investigate the impact of client advocacy on the use of analogy by novice and expert tax professionals.

The research also resulted in a published paper in which we applied our model of tax problem solving to the improvement of tax education:

- Anderson et al. (1990) reports the results of an experiment that examines the relative effectiveness of different instructional strategies in a situation in which students have prior knowledge of the topic.

SYNOPSIS OF "THE USE OF ANALOGY IN LEGAL ARGUMENT: PROBLEM SIMILARITY, PRECEDENT, AND EXPERTISE"

Legal reasoning is the construction of arguments to justify a legal position. These arguments are frequently based on decided court cases. Arguments in support of a position are constructed by drawing analogies to prior cases won by parties in similar situations. Cases that suggest contrary conclusions are distinguished by pointing out dissimilarities in the underlying legal issues. Psychological research suggests that the analogical reasoning process should be influenced not only by the "structural similarity" (shared concepts) of a decided court case and the target problem, but also by pragmatic concerns, such as client advocacy. Marchant et al. (1993) reports the results of two experiments that examine the effects of structural similarity, client advocacy, and expertise on the use of analogy in tax problem solving.

Experiment 1

Experiment 1 investigates the effects of expertise and structural similarity on the use of analogy. Experience provides tax experts with the ability to generate abstract problem representations, which makes it easier for them to identify a useful decided court case by reducing the surface-level dissimilarities between it and the target problem. This difference in problem representations between experts and novices should lead to differences in the use of analogy. If the principal concepts or structure of a decided court case are similar to those of the target problem, then experts are more likely to rely on the case than novices. On the other hand, if the decided court case does not share structural features with the target problem, but does share some surface-level details, then novices are more likely to inappropriately rely on that case.

In Experiment 1, 38 experienced professionals and 63 graduate students solved a tax problem after reading and analyzing three decided court cases. The use of analogy was measured by both fact and issue identification. In the control condition, all three decided court cases were unrelated to the problem. In the treatment condition, one of the cases was unrelated to the problem, one shared only surface-level details with the problem ("surface similarity case"), and one shared only structural features ("structural similarity case"). We found that both expert and novice tax professionals used the structural similarity case. There was negligible use of the surface similarity case.

Experiment 2

Client advocacy was not an issue in Experiment 1 because the outcomes of the decided court cases were always contrary to the taxpayer's interests. In the absence of pragmatic concerns, subjects in Experiment 1 relied on the structural similarity case and disregarded the surface similarity case. Pragmatic concerns were manipulated in Experiment 2 by varying the outcomes of the decided court cases, that is, whether the court ruled for or against the taxpayer. We predicted that client advocacy would alter the perceived usefulness of the structural and surface similarity cases as precedent, and thereby influence the use of analogy.

In Experiment 2, 128 professionals and 146 students solved a tax problem after reading and analyzing four decided court cases. The cases consisted of a structural similarity case, a surface similarity case, and two cases that were unrelated to the target problem. Pragmatic concerns were manipulated by varying whether the decided court cases contained rulings that were for or against the taxpayer. We found that the use of both the structural and the surface similarity cases varied, depending on whether the court ruled for or against the taxpayer. For example, the subjects were more likely to use the structural similarity case when the court ruled for the taxpayer.

Discussion

The results of Experiment 2 support the predicted effects of client advocacy on the use of both the structural and surface similarity cases. Overall, the results of Experiments 1 and 2 suggest that pragmatic considerations override similarity constraints in the use of analogy in the tax setting.

THE ACCOUNTING REVIEW

Although the paper was eventually published in *Organizational Behavior and Human Decision Processes* (*OBHDP*), we submitted an earlier draft of the paper for publication in *The Accounting Review* (*TAR*). Therefore, the tale of how we wrote and published this paper begins with an account of how the paper was rejected by *TAR*.

We conducted our empirical work and drafted the initial manuscript in late 1988 and early 1989. In March 1989, we submitted the manuscript to *TAR*. This draft reported the results of only Experiment 1, since we had not yet envisioned running Experiment 2. As discussed above, Experiment 1 investigates how a tax professional's expertise interacts with the structural and surface similarity of decided court cases in determining the use of analogy. The theory and design followed that of Novick (1988) who studied this issue in a more general psychological experiment. There were two predictions. First, experts are more likely than novices to use analogy when there is structural similarity between a decided court case and the target problem. Second, novices are more likely than experts to use an inappropriate analogy when there is surface similarity, but no structural similarity between a decided court case and the target problem. The novices were Masters in Tax students who completed the experimental materials during a regular class session. The experts were Big-Six tax accountants who completed the materials during a firm training session. Contrary to Novick's findings, in our experiment, tax expertise did not increase the use of the structural similarity case, nor did it protect against the inappropriate use of the surface similarity case.

First Set of Reviews

We received our first set of reviews in May 1989. The editor's letter began as follows.

> Attached are two review reports on your manuscript. Both reviewers recommend that the paper not be published in *The Accounting Review.* I cannot find sufficient ground on which to disagree...

Both reviewers thought that the basic research idea was interesting and had the potential to support a publishable paper. However, they also saw three serious deficiencies in the current manuscript.

Problem 1: Who cares? Both reviewers lamented that our study had no concrete implications for tax practice. Reviewer B put it this way:

> I think the authors could have helped their case by a better explanation of why this might be a fruitful study for applied tax research.

Reviewer A was more blunt.

> I fail to see the implication the authors are drawing, or would like to draw, from the results of this study.... It seems the authors are willing to say anything that sounds reasonable to justify the whole exercise.

The reviewers saw the study as a test of whether some results from a psychology experiment (Novick 1988) would replicate in the tax setting. In their minds, a mere replication was not sufficient motivation without an analysis of why Novick's results should or should not replicate in a tax context. We did not view our study as a mere replication, but instead saw it as an initial investigation of a fundamental tax judgment process as it is institutionalized in the rule of *stare decisis*.

Problem 2: I don't get it. Both reviewers also thought the manuscript was poorly written. The editor summarized these review comments as follows:

> Both [reviewers] believe that the experiment is difficult to understand and want some elaboration on what, exactly, was done.

The primary culprit was technical jargon. Our theory and experimental design were based largely on prior psychological research, and we made the mistake of also importing a lot of jargon from that literature. As a result, the reviewers did not fully understand our study and found reading the manuscript a frustrating experience.

Problem 3: Negative results. The major problem with our initial manuscript was that our empirical results did not support the hypotheses. To make matters worse, we did not provide a convincing story as to whether the flaw was in the theory or in the method. Reviewer A put it this way:

> [G]iven that their results are not significant, I believe that the authors should devote some attention to explaining why.... Although the authors spend several pages developing their hypotheses, they are very quick to abandon them based on the results of a single experiment.

Reviewer B stated the problem more simply.

> [A]s there are no results, there really doesn't seem to be a great value in the paper.

Our Response

How did we respond to the significant issues raised by the reviewers? We revised and resubmitted, of course. But we did so too quickly (within one month after receiving the reviews), and without doing any additional empirical work. In hindsight, we should have first collected additional data in order to better understand why our experiment did not provide the expected results. At that time, however, we were all untenured assistant professors. Patience was not one of our virtues.

We also misdiagnosed the problem. We convinced ourselves that the reviews were negative mainly because of a communication problem. If only we could revise the manuscript to more effectively communicate the importance of our research, the reviewers would "see the light" and recommend publication. As a result, our responses consisted of restatements of what the study was about, and suggestions as to how the reviewers may "enlighten" themselves about critical issues by reading some of the references that we supplied.

Second Set of Reviews

The reviewers were not impressed by our editorial revisions. One reviewer responded as follows:

> This is a slight revision of [the paper] which was rejected in May. I'm not sure how to take it. It seems it was submitted again rather rapidly and the fundamental problems I felt it had are still there. There have been improvements in the writing and explanation, but the research is as it was.

The other reviewer wrote.

> I am a little mystified by why the authors sent this work back so soon. I regret not liking the paper because it is in a promising area, but I had a lot of difficulty with it.

It was now clear to us that we had to fundamentally rethink how to package and sell the paper. Consistent with the reviewers' initial comments, this had to include collecting additional data and further developing the theory as it applied to the tax setting. It took us six months to gather additional data, rewrite, and resubmit the paper, but this time to another journal.

ORGANIZATIONAL BEHAVIOR AND HUMAN DECISION PROCESSES

Additional Empirical Work

The manuscript submitted to *TAR* reported the results of only Experiment 1. Client advocacy was held constant in Experiment 1 by making all of the case opinions contrary to the taxpayer's interests. Experiment 2 examined whether the inclusion of client advocacy would alter the usefulness of both cases as precedent and thereby influence the use of analogy. Overall, the results of Experiments 1 and 2 suggest that pragmatic considerations override similarity constraints in the use of analogy in the tax setting. In April 1990 we submitted the new manuscript to *OBHDP*.

First Set of Reviews

We received our first set of reviews in July 1990. The editor summarized the reviewers' evaluation of the manuscript as follows:

> Both felt that the manuscript had merit but that in its present form it was inappropriate for publication. Both felt that it needs revisions...

One lingering problem was that the theory and method were still not easily understood, despite our considerable efforts to remedy this problem. In Reviewer 1's opinion:

> There is too much jargon pretending to be scientific language...

Reviewer 2 had more significant concerns:

> I studied the manuscript for two hours, and I still don't understand some critical aspects of the method.... [T]he write-up of the present experiments left me in the dark on several key issues. If I am a representative reader of the paper, it is absolutely essential that the manuscript be revised to clarify the method and data analysis before it can be reviewed.

The root of our problem was that the design of Experiment 2 was quite complex. We examined the effects of three factors in this experiment: the outcome (for or against the taxpayer) of the surface similarity case, the outcome (for or against the taxpayer) of the structural similarity case, and expertise. Therefore, our data analysis had to accommodate three possible main effects, three two-way interactions, and one three-way interaction. To make matters worse, we had five dependents measures. These included the subject's prediction of how a court would rule regarding the target problem, and four measures of the use of analogy in making this prediction: identification of the key fact in the surface similarity case, identification of the key issue in the surface similarity case, identification of the key fact in the structural similarity case, and identification of the key issue in the structural similarity case.

Our main chore in revising and resubmitting the manuscript was to reanalyze and present our data in a simpler and more understandable format. To achieve this result, we made two basic changes. First, we converted the four fact and issue identification measures into composite measures, one for the structural similarity case and the other for the surface similarity case. Second, we revised the analysis so as to present the results of the two new analogy measures conditional on the third dependent measure, the predicted outcome of the target problem. The new presentation made the pattern of our results across the experimental conditions much clearer to the reader.

Second Set of Reviews

We received our second set of reviews from *OBHDP* in November 1990. One of the reviewers was impressed with our revisions, but the other reviewer still did not like the manuscript.

> You will see from the enclosed comments that you were able to satisfy most of the concerns of one reviewer but were less able to do so with the second reviewer. [Editor's letter]

In fact, Reviewer 1 had only a few remaining minor editorial comments. Reviewer 2, on the other hand, still had two significant problems with the manuscript. First the good news:

> This is an extremely responsive revision of the earlier draft of the manuscript that does clarify a lot of the factors that confused me on first reading.

Then the bad news:

> I think the authors have a fundamental misunderstanding of the concept of 'analogical reasoning'.... To be blunt, I think the authors of the paper do not understand what an analogical reasoning process is.

Reviewer 2 believed that the subjects were not relying on the decided court cases in making their decisions, but instead were reasoning directly from the statutes to a solution. Although manipulating the available decided court cases may have affected what statute the subjects relied on, the subjects were not mapping a solution from the decided court cases to the target problem. In Reviewer 2's mind, the latter was the essence of analogical reasoning, and there was no evidence of its presence in our study.

Our response was to revise the manuscript so as to better describe the theoretical relationship between statutes and decided court cases in legal reasoning. Statutes are typically inadequate for solving legal problems because the predicates in statutes are often ill-defined. For example, there is a tax statute that clearly provides a deduction for expenses incurred "in carrying on a trade or business." It is often unclear, however, whether a particular expenditure is related to a trade or business activity, as opposed to a personal activity. In these situations, decided court cases are used to reason analogically about the circumstances in which a statute applies. Therefore, the typical legal problem does not involve determining which statute to apply or deductively applying a particular statute. Rather, the problem is to identify the facts and issues that determine the proper application of the statute. In sum, we believed our experiments were, in fact, measuring whether subjects were relying on the decided court cases, and thereby reasoning analogically.

Having revised the manuscript yet another time, and having been given the green light by one reviewer, we hoped we were close to an acceptance. We had to wait only two weeks.

Acceptance

In February 1991 we received a letter from the editor of *OBHDP*. It said simply:

> I must thank you for the detailed response concerning the manner in which you revised the manuscript to deal with the numerous issues raised by the two reviewers. I believe that we have reached the stage where the publication of this manuscript would be appropriate. I think that you have done an excellent job of responding to the concerns of the reviewers in this latest revision and I am now accepting the manuscript for publication.

Publication

Two years after receiving the acceptance letter, and fully five years after we began the project, we finally saw our paper in print in the June 1993 issue of *OBHDP*. Although this event marked the formal end of this research, the real end to the day-to-day work came two years earlier when the paper was accepted for publication. Despite the two year wait, we savored the moment. Most attempts to publish in major journals fail. Thus, seeing one's work in print is a cause for some satisfaction.

PUBLISHING BEHAVIORAL TAX RESEARCH

My research regarding analogical reasoning in tax problem solving taught me many things about the research and publication process, including the following.

1. Do not limit your set of potential co-authors to tax faculty. In my case, behavioral audit researchers made excellent colleagues. They understand the psychological literature, know how to design and run experiments, and appreciate the challenges involved in studying professional judgment.

2. Do an in-depth review of the behavioral decision making literature before designing your experiments. Do not limit your literature review to the accounting and tax literatures. If you do, you will probably miss many studies that provide good ideas about how to formulate your theory and empirical tests. In the case of our research regarding analogical reasoning in taxation, it is difficult to see how we could have designed our experiments without the insights provided by prior psychological research.

3. Be patient during the review process. Take the time to develop full and complete responses to the reviewers' comments. Although this may require additional, time-consuming empirical work, it may save time in the long run. Resubmitting a paper that does not address the reviewers' concerns wastes a round in the review process, and may result in the rejection of a good paper that just needs some more work.

4. Good luck publishing a "no results" paper, you will need it. If the empirical results do not support the hypotheses, reviewers will demand a convincing story as to why this occurred. The flaw may be in the theory or it may be in the method. It is usually difficult to resolve these issues without positing additional hypotheses and conducting additional empirical tests. In other words, you need results.

5. Use simple, easy-to-understand language in your paper. Do not expect a good review if reading your paper is a long and frustrating experience. Also, do not assume that reviewers are familiar with technical jargon, particularly jargon imported from psychology and other base disciplines.

I hope these ideas will be useful to Ph.D. students and new faculty interested in publishing behavioral tax research.

REFERENCES

Adams, L., J. Kasserman, A. Yearwood, G. Perfetto, J. Bransford, and J. Franks. 1988. Memory access: The effects of fact-oriented versus problem-oriented acquisition. *Memory & Cognition* (March): 167–175.

Anderson, U., G. Marchant, J. Robinson, and M. Schadewald. 1990. Selection of instructional strategies in the presence of related prior knowledge. *Issues in Accounting Education* (Spring): 41–58.

Ashley, K. 1988. Arguing by analogy in law: A case-based model. In *Analogical Reasoning: Perspectives of Artificial Intelligence, Cognitive Science and Philosophy,* edited by D. Helman, 205–224. Dordrecht, The Netherlands: Kluwer.

Frensch, P., and R. Sternberg. 1989. Expertise and intelligent thinking: When is it better to know more? In *Advances in the Psychology of Human Intelligence* 5, edited by R. Sternberg, 157–188. Hillsdale, NJ: Erlbaum.

Gentner, D. 1983. Structure-mapping: A theoretical framework for analogy. *Cognitive Science* 7: 155–170.

Gick, M., and K. Holyoak. 1980. Analogical problem solving. *Cognitive Psychology* (July): 306–355.

Gick, M., and K. Holyoak. 1983. Schema induction and analogical transfer. *Cognitive Psychology* (January): 1–38.

Holland, J., K. Holyoak, R. Nisbett, and P. Thagard. 1986. *Induction: Processes of Inference, Learning and Discovery.* Cambridge, MA: MIT Press.

Holyoak, K., and P. Thagard. 1989. Analogical mapping by constraint satisfaction. *Cognitive Science* 13: 295–355.

Lockhart, R., M. Lamon, and M. Gick. 1988. Conceptual transfer in simple insight problems. *Memory & Cognition* (January): 36–44.

Marchant, G. 1989. Analogical reasoning and hypothesis generation in auditing. *The Accounting Review* (July): 500–513.

Marchant, G., J. Robinson, U. Anderson, and M. Schadewald. 1989. A cognitive model of tax problem solving. *Advances in Taxation* 2: 1–20.

Marchant, G., J. Robinson, U. Anderson, and M. Schadewald. 1991. Analogical transfer and expertise in legal reasoning. *Organizational Behavior and Human Decision Processes* (April): 272–290.

Marchant, G., J. Robinson, U. Anderson, and M. Schadewald. 1992. Analogy and tax problem solving. *Advances in Taxation* 4: 235–246.

Marchant, G., J. Robinson, U. Anderson, and M. Schadewald. 1993. The use of analogy in legal argument: Problem similarity, precedent, and expertise. *Organizational Behavior and Human Decision Processes* (June): 95–119.

Novick, L. 1988. Analogical transfer, problem similarity, and expertise. *Journal of Experimental Psychology: Learning, Memory and Cognition* 14: 510–520.

Sternberg, R. 1977. Component processes in analogical reasoning. *Psychological Review* (July): 510–520.

Part II

PROSPECTS

4

THE STATE OF BEHAVIORAL TAX RESEARCH: AN EDITOR'S PERSPECTIVE

EDMUND OUTSLAY

INTRODUCTION

My goal in this chapter is to provide you with my observations about the "state" of behavioral tax research from my perspective as editor of *The Journal of the American Taxation Association* (*JATA*) from 1990–1993. My observations focus on where behavioral tax research (BTR) has been, what distinguished "successful" papers (defined as papers accepted for publication) from unsuccessful papers during my term as editor, and some thoughts on future directions for behavioral tax researchers.

At the outset, I should state that I do not consider myself an "expert" in behavioral tax research. My formal doctoral program training was in economics and statistics, not in psychology (in fact, behavioral tax research was only a gleam in tax accounting researchers' eyes when I was a doctoral student in the late 1970s). However, due to the large volume of BTR papers submitted to *JATA* during my editorship, I was forced as the "arbiter" of "discussions" between authors and reviewers to become more knowledgeable about this line of research. I am especially indebted to the authors and reviewers of BTR papers for my education in this area.

I should also state that BTR papers were the most challenging (and frustrating) papers for me to arbitrate. As I revisit my manuscript files, I do not find it surprising that the BTR file folders are the thickest, often reflecting the lengthy discussions between authors and reviewers as to whether the topic (research contribution) was of interest to the readership and, more likely, whether the results could be attributed to the experimental manipulation. With archival-based data (e.g., Compustat or Internal Revenue Service data tapes), reviewers' requests for additional data could be fulfilled without redoing the entire research project. With experimental data, however, this was usually not the case. A "fatal flaw" in an experimental instrument almost always necessitated an entirely new round of data collection with new subjects, a process that was both time consuming and expensive, not to mention demoralizing. This "all-or-nothing" aspect of BTR led to more protracted defenses of the research design by authors.

A LOOK BACK AT BEHAVIORAL TAX RESEARCH

The term "behavioral tax research" has an "Alice-in-Wonderland" quality to it in that the words mean what a researcher says they mean. Based on a definition provided by the Chair of the Accounting, Behavior, and Organizations Section of the American Accounting Association, I use the term "behavioral" to describe the "full range of studies that attempt to explain cognition, reasoning, judgment, decision-making and action" (Ponemon 1995, 1) within the context of the tax domain. Such a definition encompasses a broad array of experimental research directed at human subjects, including experimental economics, cognitive psychology, and social psychology. The range of tax-related topics addressed by such research is also broad, including tax compliance (taxpayer and tax preparer), tax knowledge acquisition and transmission, tax professionals' judgment and decision making, and behavioral changes induced by tax incentives.

Behavioral tax research is a relatively young research paradigm, especially among tax accounting researchers. In their review of tax dissertations completed between 1967–1984, Brighton and Michaelsen (1985) did not classify a single research project as using a "laboratory-observation" experimental research design. Behavioral accounting research (BAR) began to be published in the early 1970s (see Libby (1981), Libby and Lewis (1982), Ashton (1982a), and Swieringa and Weick (1982) for a review and critique of the early BAR literature).

As early as 1973, Crumbley (1973) called for tax accounting academics to become more involved in studying the behavioral implications of tax law and policy, particularly as they related to the potential impact of proposed tax legislation. According to Crumbley, such research was needed because "most tax laws are enacted without adequate consideration of their behavioral effects"[1] (Crumbley 1973, 759). Crumbley contended that accountants were "uniquely qualified" to carry out such research because of their "familiarity with the tax laws and the financial affairs of individuals and businesses" (Crumbley 1973, 760). Crumbley did not endorse experimental research over empirical research as the preferred methodological approach to address behavioral issues; rather, he urged tax accountants to become more involved in pursuing the research topic.

Ashton (1974) pointed out in his comment to Crumbley's paper that "behavioral" research could be either "ex-ante" (laboratory) or "ex-post" (empirical) and called on Crumbley to be more specific in recommending a methodological approach to the study of tax-related behavioral issues. Ashton (1974) also stated his belief that competence in various types of research techniques was more important than competence in accounting techniques in conducting behavioral research, however defined. Crumbley (1974, 837) replied that Ashton's concern with the definition of behavioral tax research was "semantical" and rejected his "inference that tax accountants are unable to be competent in various types of research techniques."

This exchange illustrates that how individuals define "behavioral" research continues to be a many-colored coat. It also exemplifies the somewhat defensive posture taken by tax accounting academics at the "dawn" of empirical and experimental research in tax-related areas. Fortunately, future generations of tax accounting researchers pursued both types of research and proved to be highly competent in both "accounting techniques" and "research techniques."

Crumbley's call for "behavioral" tax research related to tax policy was answered somewhat slowly. The first "ex-ante" behavioral research conducted by tax accounting researchers was directed at tax policy issues related to tax incentives and appeared in print in the early 1980s. O'Neil (1982) constructed an employment decision model and used "human judgment research techniques" to evaluate whether the targeted jobs credit would encourage employers to hire the targeted employee groups. O'Neil constructed a questionnaire that was mailed to employers in various regions in Colorado and asked them to make hypothetical employment decisions regarding prospective employees based on different attributes, including the availability of the targeted jobs credit. O'Neil's research, although not conducted in a controlled "laboratory" setting, differed from prior survey research in that the research instrument incorporated the credit as a variable in the employer's decision-making *process* rather than simply ask for the employer's opinions about the credit's effectiveness (compare her

---

1. The issue as to whether and to what extent behavioral implications are taken into account when new legislation is proposed is still a hot issue today. For more discussion on this topic, see Joint Committee on Taxation (1995) and Gravelle (1995).

study with that of Porcano (1984a), who asked corporate managers for their opinions about the impact of tax incentives on their investment decisions).

White (1983) investigated whether the nontaxable treatment of certain fringe benefits was a sufficient incentive for employees to replace a portion of cash compensation with such benefits. His experimental instrument took the form of a questionnaire that was administered to 750 employees at four different organizations (it appears from the paper that the instrument was administered by the organization and not the researcher, thus depriving the researcher of control over the experimental task itself). Subjects were asked to allocate their salary between cash and non-cash benefits using percentages that added up to 100 percent. The tax variable was controlled by informing equal numbers of subjects that the benefits were either taxable or non-taxable. Formal hypotheses were tested regarding the taxability of the benefits and the subjects' job classification. MANOVA was used to analyze the statistical model (a four-by-two factorial design). White (1983) concluded that certain fringe benefits (e.g., life and health insurance) were tax insensitive, while others (e.g., legal services) were tax sensitive.

Porcano (1984b) used distributive justice theories as a framework for exploring taxpayer perceptions about tax fairness. His experimental instrument asked subjects to allocate a $100,000 tax liability to differently situated taxpayers (single and married, zero or two dependents, different income) and also asked them which "distribution rule" influenced their allocation choice. No formal hypotheses were tested, although subjects' decision making criteria were explored. The instrument was administered to students during class time and was mailed to faculty at the researcher's university. Porcano (1984b) found that subjects favored a progressive tax structure and urged Congress to consider the public's views on fairness before enacting new tax legislation.

Behavioral tax research that examined tax compliance issues was first published in the mid-1980s. Milliron (1985a, 1985b) examined how taxpayers perceived "tax complexity" and how such perceptions affected their potential reporting positions (compliance) and their sense of tax equity. Her instrument asked for "similarity judgments" on pairs of short tax scenarios, and she used multidimensional scaling techniques to identify various dimensions of perceived tax complexity. Taxpayer responses were correlated to various compliance decisions and opinions about tax equity. The instrument was administered to jurors awaiting assignment in a county court house, allowing the researcher a degree of control not afforded by a mailed survey. The research was exploratory in nature and no formal hypotheses were tested (see Daly and Omer (1990) for a critique of Milliron's analysis of her results).

Jackson and Jones (1985) attempted to determine if the threat of increased penalties or increased detection would serve as a greater deterrent to tax noncompliance using a laboratory instrument administered to students. The instrument presented subjects with various loss alternatives (contextual and noncontextual) that were equal from an expected value (utility) standpoint. The researchers tested their results using both expected utility theory and prospect theory and found that subjects were more sensitive to increased penalties (loss magnitude) than to increased detection risk. The results, while internally valid, were difficult to generalize because the instrument suffered from external validity problems (the magnitudes of the penalties and detection risk were not realistic). Such validity trade-offs continue to be an important and challenging aspect of behavioral tax research.

The first set of research papers in the area of tax professionals' judgment and decision making were published in 1988. Helleloid (1988) examined the extent to which "hindsight bias" (i.e., the proposition that individuals overestimate the extent to which they or someone else expected a now realized event) was evident in tax professionals' assessments of their "client's" pre-outcome expectation in three different cases (e.g., the client's profit expectation in a "hobby" scenario). Helleloid (1988) manipulated the outcome information (whether the outcome, such as profits, actually occurred) given to his subjects (professionals enrolled in an evening masters in tax program) and tested the hypothesis that subjects given favorable outcome information would judge their client's pre-outcome assessment of the alternative outcome as higher than subjects given unfavorable outcome information. He also tested whether subjects with favorable outcome information would recommend more aggressive reporting position than subjects with unfavorable outcome information. Helleloid (1988) did not find evidence of hindsight bias in the first case, but he did find that subjects given favorable outcomes were more aggressive in recommending a position to their clients, which Helleloid concluded was consistent with the practitioner's advocacy role.

Kaplan et al. (1988) looked at the impact of experience (defined as number of years in practice) and outcome information (defined as recent audit outcomes with the Internal Revenue Service) on tax practitioners' recommendations in unambiguous and ambiguous fact patterns. Relying on social cognition research and their own audit judgment research, the researchers hypothesized that experience would exert a stabilizing effect on recommendations and cause more experienced practitioners to be more conservative in ambiguous situations. They also hypothesized that favorable recent experiences with IRS audits would influence practitioners to be more aggressive in their recommendations. Both hypotheses were supported. In addition, Kaplan et al. (1988) found that probability of audit and probable loss due to IRS audit significantly influenced recommendations in non-ambiguous situations, suggesting that practitioners were willing to play the "audit lottery" outcome in non-ambiguous cases.

Chang and McCarty (1988) examined judgments of substantial authority made by tax practitioners (30) and tax accounting students (52) using a context-specific case study (real estate transaction) in which 35 different combinations of five client data facts were manipulated. They found high mean correlations of judgment consensus and judgment stability between tax practitioners regarding interpretations of substantial authority, but they also found a gap in judgment quality between practitioners and students. Based on their results, Chang and McCarty recommended that students not be used as surrogates for tax practitioners in expert judgment studies.

The first published behavioral tax research using experimental economics was conducted by Swenson (1988), who examined whether increased tax rates caused individual taxpayers to reduce their work effort. Student subjects were given a choice between a work task (key strokes on a computer) for which they were compensated, and a leisure task (reading a magazine or playing a computer game), for which they were not compensated. Swenson found that, on average, work effort initially increased when tax rates increased, but subsequently declined when tax rates became high (73 percent and 87 percent). The results were deemed to be consistent with supply-side economic theory, although individuals varied greatly in their specific responses to tax rate changes.[2] Davis and Swenson (1988) subsequently published a "primer" on using experimental economics in tax policy research that I recommend to anyone contemplating research in this domain (see Bonner et al. (1991) for additional insights on this methodology and Davis et al. (1995) for a recent study using this approach to study the impact of tax subsidies on research and development).

Behavioral tax research "exploded" in the latter half of the 1980s and continues unabated today. From 1988 to mid-1995, *JATA* served as the primary outlet for behavioral tax research, publishing 26 BTR main

2. To what extent high-income taxpayers respond to changes in tax rates is still a controversial issue today. More recent research on this phenomenon has been empirical rather than experimental (see, for example, Feldstein and Feenberg (1993) and Tillinger and Loudder (1994)).

articles out of a total of 70 (37 percent).[3] The second most popular outlet during this time period was *Advances in Taxation*, which published
13 BTR main articles out of a total of 54 (24 percent). Behavioral tax
research has also been published to a lesser extent in the *Accounting
Review* (8 articles), the *National Tax Journal* (2 articles), and the *Journal of
Accounting Research* (1 article). No BTR has been published to date in
Behavioral Accounting Research, although I suspect this journal will
become a more popular outlet in the future.

AN OVERVIEW OF BEHAVIORAL TAX RESEARCH SUBMITTED TO *JATA*, 1990-1993

During my term as editor of *JATA* (1990–1993), I received 130 new
manuscripts, of which 30 could be classified as behavioral tax research
(23 percent). Eleven of these 30 manuscripts were eventually accepted
for publication (36.7 percent). In addition, I inherited another four BTR
papers that were also accepted for publication. The acceptance rate for
BTR papers (which was approximately 15–20 percent) was considerably higher than that for non-BTR papers.

The 34 BTR manuscripts I received can be classified into six broad
topic areas:

- Taxpayer compliance (11)
- Judgment and decision making by tax professionals (11)
- Taxpayer perceptions of fairness and alternative tax structures (6)
- Demand for and evaluation of tax services (2)
- Tax incentives and taxpayer behavior (2)
- Tax education (2)

A wide range of issues were addressed within each topic area; these
issues are summarized in table 1. Papers subsequently published in
JATA are noted next to the topic.

TABLE 1. Summary of BTR Topics—Papers Submitted to JATA, 1990-1993.

Taxpayer Compliance	Determinants of tax compliance using a contingency model framework (Collins et al. 1992)
	Effect of prepayment amount on the amount of income tax liability reported (Dusenbury 1994)

---

3. Another four papers presented at the 1995 *JATA* Conference will be published in a forthcoming supplement to the journal.

TABLE 1. Summary of BTR Topics—Papers Submitted to JATA, 1990-1993.

	Effect of color-enhanced tax forms and instructions on taxpayers' task performance
	Effect of social stigmatization on tax compliance
	Effect of tax form redesign on taxpayer task performance
	Effects of detection risk and taxpayers' ethical posture on tax compliance (Carnes and Englebrecht 1995)
	Effect of income tax withholding on compliance using a prospect theory framework (White et al. 1993)
	Effect of practitioner recommendations on tax compliance
	Tests of tax avoidance behavior using experimental economics
	Effects of taxpayers' perceived probability of audit and ethical standards on compliance
	Effects of individual differences among taxpayers on compliance
Judgment and Decision-Making by Tax Professionals	Impact of preparer penalties and client compensation on tax preparers' levels of aggressiveness (Reckers et al. 1991)
	Effects of compensation, career investment, and audit probability on tax preparer compliance
	Effects of advocacy on preparers' evaluations of judicial evidence (Johnson 1993)
	Contextual factors (complexity, client aggressiveness, probability of IRS audit) impacting information requests by tax preparers
	Influence of economic deterrents on tax preparer recommendations
	Impact of information sets and context on tax professionals' similarity judgments in transfer pricing
	Existence of hindsight bias in application of qualitative tax return preparation standards
	Impact of economic sanctions (penalties) on tax preparers' aggressiveness (Cuccia 1994)

TABLE 1. Summary of BTR Topics—Papers Submitted to JATA, 1990-1993.

	Effect of client preference and client payment status on tax preparers' aggressiveness (Schisler 1994)
	Effectiveness of machine learning in determining decision rules for compensation planning
	Relationship of method to the efficiency and effectiveness of knowledge acquisition from tax experts
Taxpayer perceptions of fairness and alternative tax structures	Using abstract and concrete framing to understand taxpayers' preferences for tax progressivity
	Examine taxpayers' perceptions of vertical equity (Hite and Roberts 1991)
	Impact of education on perceptions of fairness
	Impact of legislative justification on perceptions of fairness (Wartick 1994)
	Effect of television ads designed to change taxpayers' perceptions of fairness (Roberts 1994)
	Evaluating taxpayer preferences for different rate structures and fairness
Demand for and evaluation of tax services	Evaluation of client perceptions of tax preparer quality using exchange theory and perception gap analysis (Christensen 1992)
	Measuring client satisfaction as a function of expectation and experience
Tax incentives and taxpayer behavior	Influence of tax incentives in assessing the attractiveness of foreign investment locations (Rolfe and White 1992)
	Impact of taxes on security pricing using experimental economics
Tax education	Use of writing exercises to enhance tax learning (Hite and Parry 1994)
	Facilitation of deductive reasoning within the tax domain

The methods used to collect data and the nature and number of research subjects used in the experiments are summarized in table 2. The predominant methods used to conduct behavioral research were mailed questionnaires/experimental instruments and "controlled lab experiments" in which the researcher was present when the subjects performed the required tasks. Approximately 90 percent of the experimental instruments used in the research were in the form of self-contained printed booklets that required the subjects to read case scenarios (vignettes) and make decisions regarding compliance, reporting, or preferred tax structure alternatives. The remaining ten percent of the experimental instruments were interactive computer programs that guided the subjects through various decision or investment scenarios.

TABLE 2. Summary of BTR Methodologies and Research Subjects—Papers Submitted to JATA, 1990-1993.

Taxpayer Compliance	Random mail survey of 700 households from telephone directories in two states (Collins et al. 1992)
	Controlled lab experiment administered to 65 "adults" (at least 30 years old) in small groups (Dusenbury 1994)
	Controlled lab experiment administered to 125 undergraduate tax students
	Questionnaire administered to 250 students and mailed to 400 households from telephone directories in two cities
	Controlled lab experiment administered to 86 subjects of various backgrounds (CPAs, taxpayers, students)
	Controlled lab experiment administered to 126 undergraduate tax students (Carnes and Englebrecht 1995)
	Controlled lab experiment administered to 81 full-time employees enrolled in evening MBA program and 175 undergraduate tax students (White et al. 1993)
	Experimental instrument mailed to 900 "small business" owners from a nationwide random sample purchased from a commercial service
Judgment and Decision-Making by Tax Professionals	Controlled lab experiment administered to 59 tax specialists attending a manager-level training session sponsored by an international accounting firm (Reckers et al. 1991)
	Questionnaire mailed to 2000 randomly selected licensed preparers in one state

**TABLE 2. Summary of BTR Methodologies and Research Subjects—
Papers Submitted to JATA, 1990-1993.**

	Controlled lab experiment administered to 109 Big-6 professionals attending in-house tax seminars (Johnson 1993)
	Controlled lab experiment administered to 66 tax professionals in seven different offices
	Controlled lab experiment administered to 77 tax professionals from a Big-6 accounting firm
	Experimental instrument mailed to 669 members of the AICPA Tax Division in one state
	Controlled lab experiment (computerized) administered to 81 tax preparers from commercial preparation services, non-CPA accountants, and Big-6 firms (Cuccia 1994)
	Controlled lab experiment administered to 125 tax preparers from various levels of CPA firms in two regions of the United States (Schisler 1994)
	Controlled lab experiment administered to eight CPA firm partners
Taxpayer perceptions of fairness and alternative tax structures	Questionnaire/instrument mailed to 900 households randomly selected from a list developed by a commercial firm (Hite and Roberts 1991)
	Controlled lab experiment administered to 437 tax accounting students
	Questionnaire administered to 296 accounting students at three universities
	Questionnaires mailed to 180 and 160 adult university staff employees
	Controlled lab experiment administered to 217 undergraduate accounting students and 229 members of a jury pool
	Controlled lab experiment (computerized) administered to 85 volunteers from nine investment clubs
Demand for and evaluation of tax services	Survey mailed to 441 clients and 31 tax preparers (Christensen 1992)
	Survey mailed to 688 clients of CPA firms

TABLE 2. Summary of BTR Methodologies and Research Subjects—
Papers Submitted to JATA, 1990-1993.

Tax incentives and tax-payer behavior	Instrument mailed to 67 individuals attending two conferences on investing in the Caribbean (Rolfe and White 1992)
	Controlled lab experiment (computerized) administered to 30 upper-division and graduate students
Tax education	Test group of 44 undergraduate students and control group of 46 undergraduate students (Hite and Parry 1994)

Subjects used in the research projects varied widely. Research addressing taxpayer compliance and taxpayer perceptions of fairness employed both "real world" taxpayers and university students. All researchers investigating judgment and decision-making issues used tax professionals at various levels. The number of subjects sought in the research projects varied widely as well, ranging from as few as eight to as many as 900. Rarely, if at all, did the researchers attempt to relate the number of subjects sought for their experiments to the power of their statistical tests; rather the number of subjects used in the project was most often a function of their availability or the researcher's budget. Researchers seeking to argue that their subjects represent a "national sample" of taxpayers or preparers sought a much larger number of participants than researchers who confined their subject pool to a particular geographic region or accounting firm. The issues of power and sample size become particularly important in exploratory studies in which the researcher attempts to identify significant variables. Authors of exploratory studies with large numbers of variables would do well to consider performing a power analysis to estimate the likelihood of a Type II error (see Cohen (1988) and Kinney (1986, 345–348) for more thorough discussions of this topic).

DISTINGUISHING "SUCCESSFUL" FROM "UNSUCCESSFUL" BEHAVIORAL TAX RESEARCH[4]

Well-done behavioral tax research, like all good research, combines the elements of a well-defined motivation, a strong theoretical framework, a tight methodology, and robust analysis, and makes an "interesting" contribution to knowledge. My observations about each of these elements follow.

Motivation and Theory

Ashton (1982b, 103) identifies "reliance on formal models or theories to guide the investigation" as one of the "hallmarks" of laboratory experimentation. The presence of a theoretical framework, or lack thereof, was a critical factor in whether a BTR paper was well-received by reviewers at *JATA*. Reviews of papers not accepted for publication often cited the paper's lack of theory or a "fuzzy" motivation. One reviewer noted that a paper's "lack of theory is not benign, as it is probably the root cause of the weaknesses in the experimental design." Another reviewer of a different study argued that the paper's hypotheses were "simply *asserted*, with no foundation. This indicates a lack of theory, and alone is sufficient to recommend rejection of the paper." A general lack of theoretical development in BTR is also identified by Shields, Solomon and Jackson (1995) in their chapter in this monograph.

Reliance on theoretical work in psychology and sociology was an important component of BTR accepted for publication during my term as editor. One reviewer of a paper not accepted for publication pointed out that the paper's literature review included nothing from the psychology or sociology literature. S(he) went on to state that:

> I think good behavioral work in tax *must* be supported by more general behavioral theories or demonstrated relationships....The point here is that we are in an applied discipline and to strengthen our research, we should be applying knowledge developed in the basic sciences to questions of interest in our discipline. Without some such foundation, the findings are subject to the criticism that we have no way of knowing if they are generalizable or serendipitous and dependent on the particular examples you have chosen.

---

4. By "successful" behavioral tax research I mean research accepted for publication at *JATA*. Some "unsuccessful" BTR submitted to *JATA* was subsequently accepted for publication at other journals.

The behavioral tax researcher must be careful when using theories from other disciplines to distinguish how the theory relates to the phenomenon of study (e.g., decision making by tax professionals). For example, in one study the researcher investigated whether tax professionals were subject to "hindsight bias" in decision-making. The study's author noted in the literature review that there was a "vast body of empirical research from psychology and applied disciplines...demonstrating that people are often unable to ignore 'disallowed' information." The reviewer pointed out that the author failed to

> explain why tax return preparers would be expected to react any differently than jurors or any of the other subjects of these hindsight bias studies. If this is a universally accepted phenomenon, why test it? Perhaps you can overcome this problem with some rewriting, for example, are there good reasons *why* we should expect tax return preparers to be able to ignore such information? However, the reasons were not apparent to me, given the extant literature on the subject.

It is incumbent that behavioral tax researchers investigating judgment and decision-making (JDM) by tax professionals relate their studies to the JDM literature in auditing. Shields, Solomon, and Jackson (1995) provide a thorough analysis of the interaction between these two areas in their chapter in this monograph.

BTR accepted for publication during my term as editor was based on a variety of theoretical frameworks, including the following:

- Judgment versus choice literature (Reckers et al. 1991)
- Exchange theory (Christensen 1992)
- Confirmatory processes (Johnson 1993)
- Prospect theory (Dusenbury 1994; White et al. 1993; Schisler 1994)
- Psychological reactance/utility maximization (Cuccia 1994)
- Information processing (Hite and Parry 1994)
- Referent cognitions theory (Wartick 1994)
- Deterrence theory (Carnes and Englebrecht 1995)

Formal hypotheses should follow from theory-driven research. As one reviewer observed, papers that lack formal hypotheses lead to the perception that the research is a descriptive study rather than an experimental study.

Methodology

Well-motivated research can be undone by a poorly constructed research design or inappropriate subjects. The result is a project that cannot be salvaged. As I reluctantly wrote to many authors:

> One of the hazards of doing behavioral research is that the researcher generally gets only one opportunity to convince the reader that the study design is sufficiently robust to justify having faith in the results. Failure to so convince the reviewers results in a completely new research study.

In my experience as editor, papers not accepted for publication (and even some that were) often were perceived as having methodological problems related to (1) method of data collection, (2) subjects tested, (3) lack of internal or external validity in the experimental design, and (4) failure to examine interaction effects, among others.

Data Collection. With respect to method of data collection, researchers used either a mailed survey or experimental instrument or used a controlled laboratory experiment. Researchers who chose to use a mailed instrument most often justified that approach by arguing that it expanded the population from which the data were collected. This was especially the case when opinions from a "national sample" were sought (see, for example, Hite and Roberts 1991).

Researchers using a mailed instrument face the daunting challenge of convincing reviewers that their responses are not contaminated by the many drawbacks associated with this technique. Alm (1991, 581) notes that surveys designed to elicit opinions and perceptions from taxpayers are subject to the following problems:

- Individuals may not remember their reporting decisions, they may not respond at all, or they may not respond truthfully (see Webley et al. (1991) for a discussion of this problem when tax compliance research is undertaken).

- Surveys are also unable to control for many relevant determinants of compliance.

- Surveys cannot determine the direction of causality between compliance and its determinants; that is, statements regarding the unfairness of a tax may result from a rationalization of noncompliance rather than be the cause of noncompliance.

Reviewers of studies using mailed instruments often pointed out the above issues and added several additional concerns. In particular, reviewers of such studies frequently questioned whether the researcher could discern whether respondents and non-respondents had the same characteristics. This was especially a concern in "national" surveys using commercial mailing lists when the researcher could not determine the characteristics of the sample to which the instrument was mailed. When taxpayers were the subjects, reviewers were rightfully concerned that the sample was overrepresented by higher-income higher-educated individuals and underrepresented by lower-income lower-educated individuals. Researchers usually tested for differences in the demographics of early and late respondents to mitigate this concern (Oppenheim 1966). When early and late respondents were similar, researchers relied on Armstrong and Overton's (1977) finding that late respondents generally had the same characteristics as non-respondents to justify the representativeness of their sample. This defense was accepted in some instances, but not in all. As Kerlinger (1986, 380) notes, "These defects [lack of response and the inability to check the responses given], especially the first, are serious enough to make the mail questionnaire worse than useless, except in highly sophisticated hands." Some reviewers have suggested the use of the randomized response methodology (Harwood et al. 1993) as a means to combat the possibility that respondents will not answer sensitive questions truthfully.

Response rates and number of respondents were also recurrent issues brought up by reviewers. Most studies that used mail surveys generated response rates between 20 and 40 percent, which is consistent with Kerlinger's (1986, 380) observation. However, most reviewers expected researchers to use the Dillman (1978) method in order to increase the response rates to 60 to 80 percent. Under the Dillman method, researchers personalize all correspondence and repeat mailings of questionnaires. Correspondence is personalized by handwriting signatures on cover letters, addressing envelopes by hand rather than by using labels, and using stamps rather than postage meters. The initial mailing is followed-up by a postcard reminder one week later, and additional questionnaires are mailed after three weeks and seven weeks. The final mailing is sent using certified mail. Examples of published BTR using a mailed instrument and the Dillman method are Hite and Roberts (1991) and Christensen (1992), which achieved response rates of 66 percent and 53 percent, respectively. Needless to say, the Dillman method is more costly and more time consuming than traditional methods of mail surveys.

Researchers using instruments that were designed to test for changes in pre- and post-treatment behavior or attitudes faced particularly daunting obstacles when sending such instruments through the mail. In particular, the researcher relinquishes control over the order in which the instrument is completed, the outside resources used, the people to whom the subject talked, and even the person who completed the instrument. As one reviewer stated in her review of such a study, "[I]t seems that we've been doing this kind of work long enough that people should have a better handle on controls and validity checks... My fear is that publishing something like this sends a message that although better controls, etc. are what the experts say to do, you can do something quick and dirty and it will still get published."

Subjects Tested. The *subjects tested* issue arose most frequently when students were used as surrogates for taxpayers in fairness and noncompliance studies. This was not an issue in the judgment and decision making research I reviewed because all such research used tax preparers as subjects. Most researchers used Ashton and Kramer (1980) to support their use of students as surrogates in decision-making studies (one researcher unsuccessfully justified his use of students by pointing out that other published studies in *JATA* had used students as subjects). Students are tempting subjects because they are accessible, fairly homogeneous demographically, and are usually willing to help their professor with a project (although in many cases they are a "captive audience" for the study).

The key issue relating to students as surrogates is generally one of relative expertise; that is, is there anything in the task context that would lead one to believe that different experiences or knowledge would lead to an expectation of different behavior? More than one reviewer questioned the use of undergraduate accounting students because they "typically lack real life experiences that are necessary to make the type of judgments" asked for. Other reviewers were concerned that students may have been "tainted" by their professors' opinions, especially if the research study involved attitudes about fairness and the instrument is administered later in the term. Some researchers (White et al. 1993) tried to overcome these potential problems by using students and non-students in their task and comparing responses to determine if they were similar. Based on my experience with reviewers, I can state that researchers were more likely to be successful in arguing that "non-traditional" students (e.g., evening class students who are older and have work experience) were acceptable surrogates for most behavioral tasks involving decision-making and attitudes.

Experimental Design. Experimental design, particularly the study's *internal and external validity*, was always a critical component of reviews of BTR. Libby (1981, 11) defines *internal validity* as the arrangement of "observations of effects and causes or treatments so that we can be sure that observed effects are the result of our treatments." He defines *exter-*

nal validity as "the ability to generalize results beyond the specific tasks, measurement methods, and actors of a specific study" (Libby 1981, 11). Shields et al. (1995, 101) use the term *natural ecology of the tax environment* to refer to external validity considerations in JDM experimental design.

Experimental researchers in an applied field such as accounting and taxation walk a fine line in trying to balance an experiment's internal and external validity. As one reviewer aptly stated: "Although experiments have the potential to enhance internal validity, it is a fact of life that it is often at the expense of external validity." While it is imperative that the researcher be able to convince the reviewer that the experimental treatments had a causal effect on the outcomes measured, it is also important that the researcher convince the reviewer that the tasks were realistic models of how individuals make decisions (e.g., how much income to report). Without the former, the results are not interpretable; without the latter, the results have little or no policy or institutional application.

Perceived violations of internal validity came in many forms in BTR I reviewed as editor (see Cook and Campbell (1979, 50–59) for a more thorough discussion of internal validity as it relates to experimental research). In some cases, researchers did not randomly assign their subjects to experimental groups or did not randomize the manner in which materials were presented to subjects (e.g., questions or the direction of a bipolar scale), thus raising the potential for an order effect (see Cuccia et al. (1995, 234–235) for a good example of how ordering effects can be dealt with in an experimental task).

In other cases, researchers did not use a control group or control case in an experiment that attempted to measure the pre- and post-effects of a particular treatment on subject behavior or attitude (see Spilker (1995) for a good example of the use of a control case in an experimental task).

Some studies were marred by the researcher's failure to administer a knowledge test to subjects before the treatment was administered. For example, if a researcher was attempting to determine how a potential tax law change would affect subjects' economic situations, it would seem imperative to include a knowledge and validity check in the instrument to determine whether the respondents understood the tax laws (e.g., what a standard deduction and itemized deduction were) and whether the responses were consistent (e.g., did subjects claim to be hurt by the loss of the mortgage interest deduction while also reporting they used the standard deduction). Knowledge tests would also be appropriate in experiments looking at judgment and decision-making issues (e.g., were reporting decisions related to "substantial authority" issues due to the phenomenon of interest or ignorance of the appropriate standards). In their recent study investigating tax professionals' aggressiveness in reporting positions, Cuccia et al. (1995) included a series of manipulation checks to determine if subjects actually perceived the vignettes as representing aggressive or conservative positions.

Reviewers expressed concerns about the researcher's failure to mask the experimental manipulation, resulting in the potential bias that subjects responded based on what they felt the "answer" should be (e.g., the amount of tax evaded) rather than on how they would react. Occasionally researchers masked their experimental manipulation too well, resulting in reviewers' conclusions that the resulting task did not relate to the phenomenon of interest.

External validity criticisms often arose in two situations: (1) the task (e.g., evaluating "substantial authority") was not "realistic" (e.g., the subject was asked to count sources of tax authority rather than evaluate facts, etc.), or (2) the treatment levels (e.g., audit probability or penalty, percentage of high-income taxpayers) were unrealistic. The first criticism usually arose because the task did not comport with the reviewer's professional experience. Shields et al. (1995) suggest that one way to address this concern is for researchers to do more pre-experimental field studies that examine how tax professionals perform their tasks and what information they consider important (see Bonner et al. (1992), Spilker (1995), and Cloyd (1995) as examples).

The second criticism is more problematic. Because actual detection rates and monetary penalties are low, use of "realistic" treatments are almost certainly going to have little or no effect on the subjects, resulting in a loss of internal validity due to weak experimental treatment. Some researchers have begun to allow subjects to guesstimate their own detection rates (Carnes and Englebrecht 1995), but this approach, while potentially fruitful, brings with it self-selection problems that threaten internal validity.

Testing for Main Effects or Interactions. In their evaluation of JDM tax research to date, Shields et al. (1995, 103) found that 92 percent of the hypotheses tested were concerned with the *main effects* of individual or task characteristics, while only 8 percent were directed at individual-by-task *interactions*. This observation is consistent with my experience reviewing such papers. As JDM tax research matured (i.e., most of the "low hanging fruit" was picked), reviewers became much more concerned when researchers failed to examine interaction effects (e.g., knowledge and audit probability, client-type and penalty). More recent JDM studies (Cuccia 1994) have begun to focus on interactions to explain heretofore "puzzling" research results (e.g., tax preparers' reporting decisions do not appear to be influenced by increases in audit probabilities). Future researchers must carefully consider interaction effects when designing JDM studies (see Spilker (1995) for an example of recent JDM research that looks at the interaction of time pressure and knowledge as they affect a tax researcher's ability to locate relevant authority in doing tax research).

SOME THOUGHTS ON FUTURE DIRECTIONS FOR BEHAVIORAL TAX RESEARCHERS

As I mentioned at the outset, I profess no special expertise in behavioral tax research. My thoughts about future directions for BTR are those of an outside observer, not one who is in the "trenches" like the authors of other chapters in this monograph.

As with all research, the researcher must consider what is her or her comparative advantage as an "accountant" doing BTR. In the JDM arena, we have better access to tax preparers, taxpayers, and even the Internal Revenue Service and have a better understanding of the institutions and technical tax laws that affect the tax reporting decision. As a result, we should be able to develop more realistic controlled experiments (i.e., injecting more "mundane realism" in the vignettes used). As the "big tators" in tax JDM are harvested, the focus will be on tighter research designs and more realistic experiments. Shields et al. (1995) do an outstanding job identifying the "orchards" left to harvest in JDM research in tax. As members of an applied science, we will be at a comparative disadvantage vis a vis economists, psychologists, and sociologists with respect to basic theory development and analytic modeling.

Although BTR is maturing (especially taxpayer compliance research), there are many research questions of interest that can be addressed with experimental research. With respect to the tax accounting profession, there exist issues related to (1) client demands and client perceptions of quality (can expectations and realizations be measured at different times); (2) the acquisition and transfer of tax expertise; (3) the relation between client attributes and the tax preparer's propensity to be aggressive (risk management); and (4) the assessment of substantial authority and reasonable basis by IRS agents (this is a real challenge).

Tax administrators appear to be searching for answers to the following questions: (1) Is the use of the carrot or the stick likely to achieve a voluntary compliance rate of 90 percent by the year 2000; (2) how do IRS agents acquire tax expertise; (3) what is the preparer's impact on taxpayer aggressiveness (exploiter vs. enforcer); (4) what is the role of morality versus "rationality" in the tax compliance decision (ethics measurements have been difficult to quantify); and (5) what are the likely taxpayer behavioral responses to tax rate increases or decreases.

As I observed earlier, I believe that controlled laboratory experiments are much preferred over surveys or mailed instruments in conducting BTR, primarily because the researcher has so much more control over how subjects perform the task. Slemrod (1992, 7) recognizes the value of such experiments in contributing to our understanding of the tax reporting process:

> Social scientists are often envious of the physical scientist's ability to conduct controlled experiments. It is unlikely, however, that the IRS will ever be able to, in the interest of the advancement of knowledge and better policy making, conduct five different enforcement policies in five different, but similar, states over an extended time. Social scientists can, however, conduct controlled experiments in a laboratory environment, and such work has yielded impressive results in fields such as strategic behavior and decision making under uncertainty.

Alm, Jackson, and McKee (1992, 315) make a similar observation:

> The laboratory has been found to be a useful device for investigating individual behavior because it allows considerable control over incentives and the institutional setting that face subjects...The absence of controlled field data—and the small chance that such data will soon be available—makes it likely that laboratory methods offer the best opportunity to investigate the individual behavioral responses to government policies.

Despite its virtues, experimental research is not without its pitfalls, and inexperienced researchers in this area would do well to consider the potential "fatal flaws" in their research design that I discussed in the previous section.

For researchers, the challenge in this area is to develop more robust theories and models in tax accounting behavioral research. Much of the BTR submitted to *JATA* while I was editor was criticized as lacking motivation and a strong theoretical basis. Too often, reviewers perceived the research as a fishing expedition or criticized the research for relying too much on prior work (i.e., there was no critical analysis whether such prior research was valid). Researchers will also be challenged to use more innovative methods (e.g., process tracing or verbal protocols) in determining how taxpayer or tax preparer behavior can be affected (Carroll 1992). An even bigger challenge will be to investigate the role of the Internal Revenue Service (the "third leg" of the tax stool) in the tax reporting process (Roberts (1995) has begun to make inroads in this area).

The growing interest in understanding how tax expertise is acquired and transferred is evidenced by the fact that the 1997 *Journal of Accounting Research* Conference is devoted to "Experts and the Application of Expertise in Accounting, Auditing and Tax." The announcement for the conference lists the following research topics as being appropriate:

- Distinguishing features of novices and experts; the existence of performance differences (and the sources of those differences) *between* experts and novices and *among* experts;
- The impact of economic incentives and other environmental influences on expert judgments and decisions;
- Expertise acquisition, and the returns to investments in expertise;
- Tests of rationality in expert judgments and decisions; deviations from theoretically optimal decision rules; and
- The role of expertise in regulation.

Lastly, given that BTR is so interdisciplinary, I strongly recommend that tax accounting researchers in this area join groups such as the Society for Judgment and Decision Making and the Accounting, Behavior, & Organizations section of the American Accounting Association. Successful behavioral tax researchers will be those who can take the generic theories provided in the behavioral sciences and apply them to the uniqueness of the tax domain.

ACKNOWLEDGMENTS

Thanks to all of the authors and reviewers who provided me with their insights and expanded my knowledge and horizons during my term as editor of *JATA*. Special thanks to Bryan Cloyd, Julie Collins, Andy Cuccia, Jon Davis, Peggy Hite, Betty Jackson, Mike Schadewald, Mike Roberts, John Robinson, and Rich White, whose work and constructive approach to reviewing I greatly admire.

REFERENCES

Alm, J. 1991. A perspective on the experimental analysis of taxpayer reporting. *The Accounting Review* 66 (July): 577–593.

Alm, J., B. Jackson, and M. McKee. 1992. Deterrence and beyond: Toward a kinder, gentler IRS. In *Why People Pay Taxes*, edited by J. Slemrod, 311–329. Ann Arbor, MI: The University of Michigan Press.

Armstrong, J., and T. Overton. 1977. Estimating nonresponse bias in mail surveys. *Journal of Marketing Research* 14 (August): 396–402.

Ashton, R. 1974. Behavioral implications in taxation: A comment. *The Accounting Review* 49 (October): 831–833.

Ashton, R., and S. Kramer. 1980. Students as surrogates in behavioral research: Some evidence. *Journal of Accounting Research* 18 (Spring): 269–277.

Ashton, R. 1982a. *Human Information Processing in Accounting, Studies in Accounting Research #17*. Sarasota, FL: American Accounting Association.

Ashton, R. 1982b. Discussion of an assessment of laboratory experiments in accounting. *Journal of Accounting Research* 20 (Supplement): 102–107.

Bonner, S., J. Davis, and B. Jackson. 1991. Frontiers in experimental tax research: Experimental economics and tax professional judgment. In *A Guide to Tax Research Methodologies*, edited by C. Enis, 42–80. Sarasota, FL: American Accounting Association.

Bonner, S., J. Davis, and B. Jackson. 1992. Expertise in corporate tax planning: The issue identification stage. *Journal of Accounting Research* 30 (Supplement): 1–28.

Brighton, G., and R. Michaelsen. 1985. Profile of tax dissertations in accounting: 1967–1984. *The Journal of the American Taxation Association* 6 (Spring): 76–91.

Carnes, G., and T. Englebrecht. 1995. An investigation of the effect of detection risk perceptions, penalty sanctions, and income visibility on tax compliance. *The Journal of the American Taxation Association* 17 (Spring): 26–41.

Carroll, J. 1992. How taxpayers think about their taxes: Frames and values. In *Why People Pay Taxes*, edited by J. Slemrod, 43–66. Ann Arbor, MI: The University of Michigan Press.

Chang, O., and T. McCarty. 1988. Evidence on judgment involving the determination of substantial authority: Tax practitioners vs. students. *The Journal of the American Taxation Association* 10 (Fall): 26–39.

Christensen. A. 1992. Evaluation of tax services: A client and preparer perspective. *The Journal of the American Taxation Association* 14 (Fall): 60–87.

Cloyd, C. 1995. Prior knowledge, information search behaviors, and performance in tax research tasks. *The Journal of the American Taxation Association* (forthcoming).

Cohen, J. 1988. *Statistical Power Analysis for the Behavioral Sciences*. Hillsdale, NJ: Lawrence Erlbaum.

Collins, J., V. Milliron, and D. Toy. 1992. Determinants of tax compliance: A contingency approach. *The Journal of the American Taxation Association* 14 (Fall): 1–29.

Cook, T., and D. Campbell. 1979. *Quasi-Experimentation: Design & Analysis Issues for Field Studies*. Boston, MA: Houghton Mifflin Company.

Crumbley, D. 1973. Behavioral implications of taxation. *The Accounting Review* 48 (October): 759–763.

Crumbley, D. 1974. Behavioral implications of taxation: A reply. *The Accounting Review* 49 (October): 834–837.

Cuccia, A. 1994. The effects of increased sanctions on paid tax preparers: Integrating economic and psychological factors. *The Journal of the American Taxation Association* 16 (Spring): 41–66.

Cuccia, A., K. Hackenbrack, and M. Nelson. 1995. The ability of professional standards to mitigate aggressive reporting. *The Accounting Review* 70 (April): 227–248.

Daly, B., and T. Omer. 1990. A comment on "A behavioral study of the meaning and influence of tax complexity." *Journal of Accounting Research* 28: 193–197.

Davis, J., and C. Swenson. 1988. The role of experimental economics in tax policy research. *The Journal of the American Taxation Association* 10 (Fall): 40–59.

Davis, J., H. Quirmbach, and C. Swenson. 1995. Income tax subsidies and research and development spending in a competitive economy: An experimental study. *The Journal of the American Taxation Association* (forthcoming).

Dillman, D. 1978. *Mail and Telephone Surveys: The Total Design Method.* New York: John Wiley and Sons.

Dusenbury, R. 1994. The effect of prepayment position on individual taxpayers' preferences for risky tax-filing options. *The Journal of the American Taxation Association* 16 (Spring): 1–16.

Feldstein, M., and D. Feenberg. 1993. Higher tax rates with little revenue gain: An empirical analysis of the Clinton tax plan. *Tax Notes* (March 22): 1653–1657.

Gravelle, J. 1995. Behavioral feedback effects and the revenue estimating process. Working paper.

Harwood, G., F. Larkins, and J. Martinez-Vazquez. 1993. Using a randomized response methodology to collect data for tax compliance research. *The Journal of the American Taxation Association* 15 (Fall): 79–92.

Helleloid, R. 1988. Hindsight judgments about taxpayers' expectations. *The Journal of the American Taxation Association* 9 (Spring): 31–46.

Hite, P., and M. Roberts. 1991. An experimental investigation of taxpayer judgments on rate structure in the individual income tax system. *The Journal of the American Taxation Association* 13 (Fall): 47–63.

Hite, P., and R. Parry. 1994. A study of the effectiveness of writing exercises as elaboration techniques for teaching tax. *The Journal of the American Taxation Association* 16 (Spring): 172–186.

Kaplan, S., P. Reckers, S. West, and J. Boyd. 1988. An examination of tax reporting recommendations of professional tax preparers. *Journal of Economic Psychology* 9: 427–443.

Kerlinger, F. 1986. *Foundations of Behavioral Research*. New York, NY: Holt, Rinehart and Winston, Inc.

Kinney, W., Jr. 1986. Empirical accounting research design for Ph.D. students. *The Accounting Review* 61 (April): 338–350.

Jackson, B., and S. Jones. 1985. Salience of tax evasion penalties versus detection risk. *The Journal of the American Taxation Association* 6 (Spring): 7–17.

Johnson, L. 1993. An empirical investigation of the effects of advocacy on preparers' evaluations of judicial evidence. *The Journal of the American Taxation Association* 15 (Spring): 1–22.

Joint Committee on Taxation. 1995. *Methodology and issues in the revenue estimating process* (JCX-2-95, January 23).

Libby, R. 1981. *Accounting and Human Information Processing: Theory and Applications*. Englewood Cliffs, NJ: Prentice–Hall, Inc.

Libby, R., and B. Lewis. 1982. Human information processing research in accounting: The state of the art in 1982. *Accounting, Organizations, and Society*: 231–286.

Milliron, V. 1985a. A behavioral study of the meaning and influence of tax complexity. *Journal of Accounting Research* 23 (Autumn): 794–816.

Milliron, V. 1985b. An analysis of the relationship between tax equity and tax complexity. *The Journal of the American Taxation Association* 7 (Fall): 19–33.

O'Neil, C. 1982. The targeted jobs credit: An evaluation of its impact on the employment decision process. *The Journal of the American Taxation Association* 3 (Winter): 15–22.

Oppenheim, A. 1966. *Questionnaire Design and Attitude Measurement*. New York: Basic Books.

Ponemon, L. 1995. Message from the chair. *The ABO Reporter* 11 (Winter): 1.

Porcano, T. 1984a. The perceived effects of tax policy on corporate investment intentions. *The Journal of the American Taxation Association* 6 (Fall): 7–19.

Porcano, T. 1984b. Distributive justice and tax policy. *The Accounting Review* 59 (October): 619–636.

Reckers, P., D. Sanders, and R. Wyndelts. 1991. An empirical investigation of factors influencing tax practitioner compliance. *The Journal of the American Taxation Association* 13 (Fall): 30–46.

Roberts, M. 1994. An experimental approach to changing taxpayers' attitudes towards fairness and compliance via television. *The Journal of the American Taxation Association* 16 (Spring): 67–86.

Roberts, M. 1995. The influence of contextual factors on IRS agents' assessments of taxpayer negligence. *The Journal of the American Taxation Association* (forthcoming).

Rolfe, R., and R. White. 1992. Investors' assessment of the importance of tax incentives in locating foreign export-oriented investment: An exploratory study. *The Journal of the American Taxation Association* 14 (Spring): 39–57.

Schisler, D. 1994. An experimental examination of factors affecting tax preparers' aggressiveness—a prospect theory approach. *The Journal of the American Taxation Association* 16 (Fall): 124–142.

Shields, M., I. Solomon, and K. Jackson. 1995. Experimental research on tax professionals' judgment and decision making. In *Behavioral Tax Research: Prospects and Judgment Calls*, edited by J. Davis, 77-126. Sarasota, FL: American Taxation Association.

Slemrod, J. 1992. Why people pay taxes: Introduction. In *Why People Pay Taxes*, edited by J. Slemrod, 1-8. Ann Arbor, MI: The University of Michigan Press.

Spilker, B. 1995. The effects of time pressure and knowledge on key word selection behavior in tax research. *The Accounting Review* 70 (January): 49–70.

Swenson, C. 1988. Taxpayer behavior in response to taxation: An experimental analysis. *Journal of Accounting and Public Policy* 7 (Spring): 1–28.

Swieringa, R., and K. Weick. 1982. An assessment of laboratory experiments in accounting. *Journal of Accounting Research* 20 (Supplement): 56–101.

Tillinger, J., and M. Loudder. 1994. Evidence of taxpayer behavioral responses to higher tax rates. *Tax Notes* (October 17): 361–369.

Wartick, M. 1994. Legislative justification and the perceived fairness of tax law changes: A referent cognitions theory approach. *The Journal of the American Taxation Association* 16 (Fall): 106–123.

Webley, P., H. Robben, H. Elffers, and D. Hessing. 1991. *Tax Evasion: An Experimental Approach*. New York, NY: Cambridge University Press.

White, R. 1983. Employee preferences for nontaxable compensation offered in a cafeteria compensation plan: An empirical study. *The Accounting Review* 58 (July): 539–561.

White, R., P. Harrison, and A. Harrell. 1993. The impact of income tax withholding on taxpayer compliance: Further empirical evidence. *The Journal of the American Taxation Association* 15 (Fall): 63–78.

5

EXPERIMENTAL RESEARCH ON TAX PROFESSIONALS' JUDGMENT AND DECISION MAKING

MICHAEL D. SHIELDS, IRA SOLOMON, AND K. DIANNE JACKSON

Since the 1980s, considerable resources have been devoted to behavioral research in tax. One subset of this research has focused on the tax professional and his or her judgment formulation and decision making (hereafter, JDM). While other persons in the tax context could be studied (e.g., the taxpayer,[1] the tax regulator), tax professionals are important if for no other reason than they are the preparers of approximately 50% of all tax returns in the United States (IRS 1987). Tax professionals, of course, also act as advisors in planning situations. The consequences, at a general level, of tax professionals' involvement in compliance and planning situations, and, more specifically, the role and impact of their JDM processes, however, still are little understood. Since, as discussed later, the essence of much of what tax professionals do is judgment formulation and decision making, it is appropriate that research be focussed on tax professionals' JDM. As also discussed later, conducting research on tax professionals' JDM requires specialized knowledge of taxation, the various tax institutions, and JDM theories and research methods. There is, therefore, considerable opportunity for accounting researchers to employ such knowledge to contribute to

1. For reviews of the research on taxpayers, see Fischer, Wartick, and Mark (1992) and Jackson and Milliron (1986).

the advancement of taxation theory and practice. Further, tax education and JDM in non-tax accounting settings, as well as other non-
accounting settings, could benefit from enhanced efforts by accounting
researchers specializing in tax.

There are five primary objectives of this chapter. The first objective
is to introduce some basic notions about JDM and JDM research in tax
and non-tax contexts and to discuss potential contributions of JDM
research to increasing tax knowledge and understanding, and improving tax practice and education. A second objective is to develop a process model of tax professionals' JDM. A third objective is to describe
JDM research frameworks and types of evaluation criteria germane to
JDM research. A fourth objective is to classify and describe the extant
experimental research on tax professionals' JDM by reference to the
previously introduced tax JDM process and JDM research frameworks.
Subsequently, we pursue the final objective: To critically analyze the
extant research on tax professionals and offer suggestions for future
research. Concluding remarks in section six complete the paper.

JUDGMENT AND DECISION-MAKING RESEARCH

The essence of much of the work performed by tax professionals is formulating judgments and making decisions. These judgments and decisions, depending on the rank of the tax professional, include, for
example, deciding client solicitation and engagement strategies, information search decisions, evaluative judgments about the relevance of
information, judgments about what advice to offer a client and how to
present the advice to the client, justifications of judgments and decisions, and deciding what to disclose to the tax agency and how to disclose it. Since these judgments and decisions are such an important
and pervasive part of the tax professionals' job, it is appropriate that
researchers seek to describe, understand, and predict them. As expli-
cated later, such research can have several purposes, including identifying how and how well tax judgments are formulated and decisions
are made.

The term *judgment* is used herein to refer to the process of estimating
outcomes and related consequences (Libby 1981). Consistently, a judgment is either an estimate of a quantity (e.g., estimate of an expected
tax liability), an evaluation of a stimulus relative to a standard (e.g., an
assessment of whether certain authoritative support exceeds the substantial authority standard), or a comparison of one stimulus to
another stimulus (e.g., the comparison of the facts and circumstances
of a court case to a client's facts and circumstances). On the other hand,

the term *decision-making* refers herein to the process of identifying and evaluating potential choice/action consequences and, as used herein, the term "decision" refers to the selected choice or action.[2] There is, of course, a link between judgments and decision—judgments coupled with "preferences" are the inputs to decision-making.

Like many accountancy settings, judging and deciding are pervasive in the daily work activities of tax professionals. Tax JDM, however, differs from financial and managerial accounting and auditing JDM in several important respects. To illustrate, in comparison to auditing, tax JDM generally requires greater forward (as opposed to backward or diagnostic) reasoning and more attention to problem identification and solution (Bonner, Davis, and Jackson 1992). There also are different information search and documentation rules in the tax setting. For example, tax professionals act as advocates for clients and, hence relative to auditors, are less interested in searching for "truth" (e.g., searching for information to perform an unbiased test of an hypothesis about the financial condition of a client). Instead, the tax professional searches for information to defend a tax treatment that is maximally advantageous to the client, and his or her information search process is more focussed on identifying evidence to support the desired treatment.

Collectively, the distinctive features of tax settings have important implications for how JDM processes should be operationalized as well as for what knowledge and skills may be required for expertise. For example, in auditing and management consulting, industry expertise typically plays an important role in determining the quality of judgments and decisions, whereas, industry knowledge generally has a smaller impact on the quality of tax professionals' JDM. We maintain, therefore, that it often will be inappropriate to simply transfer into the tax context JDM research findings developed outside that context. A short digression provides further insight into the basis for this conclusion.

JDM processes may be regarded as a function of the task/context, the information processor, and the interaction of the task/context and the processor.[3] Further, the task/context may be decomposed into content and structure (Einhorn and Hogarth 1981). Consistently, two types of tasks/contexts may be distinguished—generic and applied. The

2. Decision-making also may be viewed as the choice of a stimulus from a set of stimuli (e.g., choice of whether a taxable entity should be organized as a corporation, limited partnership or general partnership) and, under this view, the chosen stimulus is the decision.

3. The remainder of this section is based on a similar discussion in Solomon and Shields (1995).

former task/context is one in which structure is emphasized by the researcher (and content de-emphasized). On the other hand, an applied task/context is one in which both structure and content are important. While research representations of both generic and applied tasks require both structural abstraction and content simplification, the level of content abstraction is greater in the case of generic tasks relative to applied tasks.

It also is useful to distinguish between experienced and inexperienced processors, thus, resulting in four task/context-processor combinations. Much of the JDM literature has employed either a generic task/context and used inexperienced (student) subjects or an applied task/context using experienced subjects (e.g., weather forecasting by trained meteorologists). The other two combinations are not as popular, although studies using these task/context-processor combinations can make valuable contributions by increasing knowledge with respect to the incremental effects of tasks and processors on JDM processes and outcomes. An example is a JDM study in which students perform an applied task providing a baseline for identifying experience effects.

Applied task/context studies, such as tax JDM studies, have provided numerous insights into the effects of task/context structures on JDM. Contexts investigated include meteorology, medicine, juries, and auditing. Each context has numerous structural features, many of which are common to other contexts. Importantly, however, it is *not* the individual structural features but the ensemble of such structural features which distinguish one context from other contexts. In tax, these structural features include the (advisory) nature of the tax professional's role, the existence of a vigilant external monitor (i.e., the IRS), the central role of risk assessment, multiperson interaction and multiperiod consequences, ambiguous reporting rules, uncertain penalties, and the rarity of timely outcome feedback. Because accounting researchers specializing in tax not only understand tax content but have the greatest knowledge of these structural features, it is such researchers who have a comparative advantage in conducting tax JDM research.

Structural features including those just mentioned not only provide a *raison d'être* for tax JDM research as opposed to, say, audit JDM research, but make tax tasks/contexts rich testing grounds for JDM theories. For example, testing generic JDM theories in the tax context can provide evidence of the generalizability of JDM theories to different task/context structures, when consistent results are reported in tax and non-tax JDM studies. Similarly, inconsistent results in tax and non-tax JDM studies can provide evidence on the boundary conditions of generic JDM theories. Importantly, in addition to tax content and structural feature knowledge, tax researchers must understand JDM theory and be able to design and execute highly-controlled experiments if the impact of such structural features is to be convincingly isolated.

We believe that researchers may conduct tax JDM studies for four reasons. First, via JDM research, one can describe *how* and *how well* tax professionals formulate judgments and make decisions. In turn, one can learn how to *improve* tax professionals' JDM via tax JDM research. Learning how tax professionals' judgments and decisions *should be made* is a third potential reason for conducting tax JDM research. A final objective is *educational*: the process and product of tax research may be used to increase students', tax professionals', the tax research-ers', and other tax professors' knowledge. Most of the existing tax JDM research has addressed how tax professionals formulate judgments and make decisions. To a more limited extent, the question of how well these judgments are formulated and decisions are made has been addressed. Finally, the extant tax JDM research has given little atten-tion to education and JDM improvement objectives. This situation may be attributable to the infancy of this literature. On the other hand, con-siderable research opportunities are highlighted by the limited atten-tion to some of the ways in which tax JDM research can contribute.

TAX PROFESSIONALS' JUDGMENT AND DECISION MAKING

When describing tax professionals' JDM, it is useful to begin by devel-oping a framework for structuring tax tasks and the process tax profes-sionals use to formulate judgments and/or make decisions. We first define and distinguish two important classes of tax JDM tasks— open- and closed-fact tasks, and describe how within each phase of the tax professionals' JDM the cognition is likely to differ between them. We also explain why the relevant information for judgment formulation and decision-making depends on whether the tax professional is per-forming an open- or closed-fact task.

Classes of Tax JDM Tasks

A *closed-fact task* is one in which the client's tax liability arises from an extant legally binding and enforceable contract and/or transaction (Norwood et al. 1979; Raabe, Whittenburg, and Bost 1993; Sommerfeld and Streuling 1981). For expositional purposes, we assume that the tax professional's goal is to identify, develop, recommend, and defend a tax treatment that minimizes a client's expected disutility[4] subject to the tax professional maximizing his or her expected utility (e.g., profit) from the present and all other existing and potential clients. Such max-imization includes managing his or her reputation for future interactions with the present and other (potential) clients, the IRS and other regulatory and judicial agencies, and professional colleagues. To optimize such an objective function, a tax professional must consider a broad array of information including tax information applicable to the contract and/or transaction, potential regulatory penalties and their probabilities of occurrence, the client's risk preference, the tax professional's preparation cost and demand schedules, his or her risk preference, and professional constraints.

An *open-fact*, or *controllable-fact*, *task* exists when a tax professional becomes involved before a contract and/or transaction has become legally binding or enforceable against a taxpayer. For expositional convenience, we assume that in such a situation the tax professional's goal is to identify, develop, recommend, and defend the client's personal and/or business investment, financing, and/or operating contract(s) and/or transaction(s) and associated tax treatment(s) which maximize the client's expected utility (e.g., profit, net of total tax costs). Of course, this client utility maximization is subject to the tax professional maximizing his or her expected utility (e.g., profit) from the present and all other existing and potential clients (Scholes and Wolfson 1992). Also, as with closed-fact tasks, the tax professional is concerned with maximizing or managing his or her reputation. Thus, the major distinction between open- and closed-fact situations is that, in addition to the information considered in a closed-fact situation, the tax professional in an open-fact situation must consider how tax costs and their associated probabilities interact with the benefits, costs and associated probabilities for potential personal and/or business investing, financing, and/or operating contracts and/or transactions.

Thus, the goal and relevant information set are likely to differ for open- and closed-fact situations. As will be discussed shortly, this conclusion implies that different phases of the JDM process will be key, and, consequently, the importance of specific components of the tax professional's psychological processes may be expected to vary depending on whether he or she faces an open- or closed-fact situation. In particular, we will argue that when facing an open-fact situation, "constructive" psychological processes are relatively more important determinants of the tax professional's success, whereas for a closed-fact situation, "reductive" psychological processes are relatively more important.

---

4. A client's expected disutility is a function of the total tax cost (sum of the present values of the tax assessment, penalties, interest, and tax preparation expenses) and his or her risk and effort preferences.

The Tax JDM Process

Describing, understanding, and predicting tax professionals' JDM is facilitated by a pictorial representation of key activities and their sequence. Figure 1 is a parsimonious representation which, although based on a generic JDM process, is sufficient to achieve our objectives of classifying, describing and analyzing experimental tax JDM research.[5] Before describing the specific phases of this model, it is appropriate to discuss three of its characteristics.

First, the tax JDM process often takes place in a multiperson setting. In fact, in practice, much of the process may be delegated by a higher-ranking to a lower-ranking tax professional. However, extant tax JDM studies have not incorporated this feature of natural tax settings. For this reason as well as for purposes of simplification, our process model is couched in terms of individual JDM. Later, in section five, we will discuss multiperson JDM in tax settings.

Second, as with many problem-solving processes, tax JDM is iterative. At any phase of the process, the tax professional may decide that it is necessary to go back to a previous phase to obtain additional information either from the client or from additional authoritative information search. In later phases of the process, the tax professional may identify additional alternatives which need to be integrated into the original alternative ranking structure. The arrows in Figure 1 illustrate the iterative nature of the process. For discussion purposes, the process has been decomposed into distinct phases. In practice, however, it may not be easy to distinguish each phase as it is performed, the phases may occur out of order relative to Figure 1, some may be skipped entirely, and/or some phases may be performed simultaneously. Again, the distinctions among the phases of the process and their linear representation with feedback loops have been made salient for expositional purposes.

Third, we assume that a tax professional's JDM process occurs within a cognitive structure called a *mental model* (sometimes also referred to as a script or frame). A mental model is an internal representation of an external event or phenomenon (Abelson 1981; Minsky 1975; Schank and Abelson 1977; Johnson-Laird 1983). Formation of the mental model will be triggered by events occurring in the first phase of the process. Initially, the mental model will contain the state of knowledge immediately prior to problem solving and the goal state(s). *Constructive cognitive processes*, such as identification of alternatives and

---

5. Similar models of the tax JDM process were developed by Marchant et al. (1989) and Magro (1995). Both of these models greatly influenced our thinking about tax JDM.

information search, will expand the mental model, whereas *reduction processes*, such as evaluation, comparison, and selection of alternatives

FIGURE 1. The Tax Judgment and Decision Making Process .

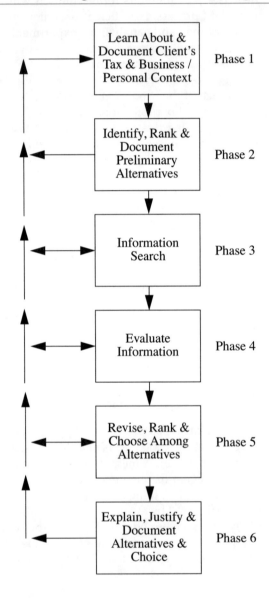

will decrease it (See Bonner and Pennington 1991). The importance of constructive and reductive processes varies between open- and closed-fact situations, and also among the six phases of the model.

Six Phases of the Tax JDM Process

During the *first phase*, the tax professional learns about the client's tax and business/personal context. When there is a new client, the tax professional and client representatives will meet so that the tax professional may learn about the client's situation and the associated facts. For a continuing client, this phase of the process effectively is ongoing and may not be directly associated with a specific open- or closed-fact situation. The tax professional will learn about a continuing client's tax and business context while working on other open- and closed-fact tasks or while interacting informally with client representatives. More specific performance will occur at this phase when the tax professional determines that a tax-related issue or opportunity exists which requires specific judgment formulation or decision-making.

The JDM process, outlined in Figure 1, may be instigated by the client, the tax professional, or other accounting professionals, such as financial-statement auditors. The client may seek out the advice of the tax professional, the tax professional may identify a closed-fact situation question (e.g.,while preparing a tax return) or an open-fact situation opportunity (e.g., during a year-end planning meeting), or the financial-statement auditors may identify a transaction with potentially significant tax consequences which previously has not been addressed. Once the process is triggered, two primary activities occur: goal determination and issue identification. This phase of the tax JDM process largely is comprised of constructive psychological processes since the tax professional's task is to generate or construct goals and identify issues. The tax professional will seek to determine and clarify the specific goals and issues of the client while developing a problem structure or frame. Goals determined at this phase will depend on whether the fact situation is open or closed. In the closed-fact situation, goal(s) primarily will be focussed on a particular tax reporting issue (e.g., determine the deductibility of a specific expense). An open-fact situation, on the other hand, is more likely to include non-tax business issues (e.g., investment, financing and operating decisions). Thus, in an open-fact situation, the goals likely will be greater in number and will have more complex interdependencies.

An important task of the tax professional is development of an information file to document his or her work activities related to the engagement and to justify and defend his or her recommendations to the client, the IRS, members of his or her firm (e.g., during the review process), and members of the public accounting profession (e.g., in the event that an ethics violation is charged). This information file will include tax and non-tax information (e.g., personal, family and business information about the client) constructed from knowledge stored in the tax professional's long-term memory and a variety of information sources (e.g., statutory law, financial statements). The tax professional will develop or revise his or her mental model of this particular client situation while actively working on the engagement. Such development or revision will be based on information retrieved from his or her long-term memory as well as information contemporaneously read from the information file and other sources of information.

Entering the *second phase* of the process, identifying and ranking preliminary alternatives, the tax professional will continue to revise his or her mental model based on new information or additional consideration of previously acquired information. This phase involves the use of constructive psychological processes to expand the mental model by identifying and ranking preliminary alternatives. For open-fact situations, this phase arguably is the most important since it is crucial to develop a relatively complete set of viable and promising contracts and/or transactions and associated tax treatments. We distinguish three primary activities during this phase—identification of alternatives, ranking of alternatives, and development of a research strategy.

First, the tax professional will identify one or more paths (alternatives) between his or her initial state of knowledge and the goal. Such identification initially will involve the tax professional retrieving relevant information from his or her memory. Importantly, in both open- and closed-fact situations, the tax professional at this stage only may have identified a small number of alternatives.

After retrieving information from memory and identifying preliminary alternatives, the tax professional will use his or her mental model to explicitly or implicitly assign a preliminary ranking to the alternatives. This ranking will be based on how well each alternative is perceived to meet the client's goals subject to meeting the tax professional's constraints mentioned earlier. Information used to develop a ranking of the alternatives also will be retrieved from the tax professional's memory.

Finally, the tax professional will use his or her mental model to design a research plan for acquiring information not in memory. This plan typically will include identification of the person to perform the search and specification of how much time should be devoted to it. The extent of the plan is likely to depend on the importance of the client, the number and complexity of the relevant tax and planning issues, and the magnitude of the potential economic impact. The tax professional will document the research plan to facilitate its justification and defense in the eyes of, primarily, the client and members of the tax professional's public accounting firm, and, secondarily, to the IRS and the accounting profession.

An important difference between open- and closed-fact situations is that, in the former, there usually is a greater range of possible alternatives. Since, in open-fact situations the contract and/or transaction has not yet been determined, the tax professional must identify alternative ways of structuring the contract and/or transaction as well as identify possible tax treatments for each possible structuring. Again, therefore, constructive psychological processes are relatively more important for open-fact situations because of the larger number of possible alternatives and interactions between contract/transaction structuring and tax treatments.[6]

Up to *phase three*, the tax professional has relied primarily on information already documented and/or retrieved from his or her memory. During the third phase, however, there is a search for information not already documented or retrievable from memory. In particular, authoritative evidence relevant to the preliminary alternatives will be obtained as well as other needed client information (e.g., business, industry). As in the prior two phases, this phase is dominated by constructive psychological processes. The amount and type of information searched will vary depending upon whether the situation is open- or closed-fact. Relative to the closed-fact situation, the open-fact situation is likely to require more extensive search due simply to the availability of a larger number of alternatives (i.e., contract and/or transaction structuring in addition to tax treatment strategy). Importantly, in addition to tax-related information, an open-fact situation may require the tax professional to obtain additional personal and business information from the client and other sources.

Phase four is the point in the tax JDM process at which reduction processes first become prominent. During this phase, the tax professional revises his or her mental model while evaluating the information already collected. The purpose of such evaluation is to determine the extent to which each alternative meets the goals and the costs and/or requirements attendant with each such alternative. A key outcome of this evaluation process is reducing the collected information to only the most relevant items. Such cognitive reduction activities may involve analogical reasoning, similarity judgments, and case-based reasoning. During this phase, the tax professional's mental model typically will be revised significantly based on his or her evaluation of

6. Non-tax legal knowledge also is pertinent to contract and transaction structuring.

information retrieved from long-term memory or acquired from external sources but now documented in the file. The end result is that the tax professional's mental model becomes smaller or parsimonious due to the consolidation of information that occurs during this phase.

Having an understanding of the relevant information, the tax professional now may be in a position to use his or her mental model to make a decision during *phase five*. Based on the evaluation of information obtained up to this point, the professional will revise the preliminary alternatives and assign final rankings if there are sufficient differences among the alternatives. If not, the tax professional will recycle to earlier phases of the tax JDM process. The choice of an alternative will be made by the client or the tax professional based on the client's preferences. However, during this decision process, the client could reveal additional information which would cause the tax professional to recycle through the JDM process. As in phase four, reduction processes play a central role in this phase. For example, based on the evaluation in phase four, the tax professional may completely eliminate some courses of action from further consideration (e.g., alternatives which are unambiguously denied by authoritative evidence). Consistently, by ranking the alternative courses of action, the tax professional naturally will focus on a subset of potential actions.

The ranking at this phase will be more sophisticated than the original ranking at phase two, if for no reason other than the professional has much more information available at this phase of the process. For example, the ranking process at phase five is likely to involve risk assessment including consideration of potential future events (e.g., tax law changes, changes in client's situation, etc.), as well as an evaluation of the strength of the authoritative support for each alternative. Not only would there be an assessment of risks to the client, but also risks to the professional and his or her firm would be assessed for each alternative. Also considered at this stage would be the likely costs, both tax and non-tax, associated with potential actions.

Differences continue at this phase between open- and closed-fact situations, specifically, in the former, there frequently are more and more complex alternatives to rank (i.e., tax treatments for closed-fact situations vs. contract and/or transaction structuring and tax treatments for open-fact situations). The open-fact situation, again, is likely to involve a greater range of potential courses of action due to the flexibility of the client's situation (i.e., generally, the absence of a legally binding contract and/or transaction will expand the scope of potential actions). Further, evaluation and ranking of the alternatives in the open-fact situation likely will be more complex since there will be non-tax as well as tax goals to consider.

During *phase six*, the tax professional will finalize documentation of the process and the decision. Importantly, the documentation will include justification for the final decision. Again, the justification is for internal purposes (i.e., the professional will need to be able to justify to superiors within his or her firm the recommendation to the client), for client purposes (i.e., the professional will need to demonstrate to the client why certain alternatives are available or not), for potential future government examination (i.e., future audit by tax authorities) as well as for the accounting profession (e.g., an ethics investigation).

In this phase, the emphasis on reduction processes is replaced by a renewed emphasis on constructive processes. That is, the tax professional must construct documentation justifying and defending the final decision for the purposes just mentioned. Documentation will be relatively complete before the alternatives are presented to the client, although the documentation may be adjusted afterward to be fully consistent with the final decision of the client. Documentation in an open-fact situation likely will be extensive since it will include a plan for future action. In a closed-fact situation, on the other hand, documentation may include certain suggestions for future action, but primarily will relate to the tax treatment of past events. In addition to differences associated with open- versus closed-fact situations, documentation will vary across engagements as a result of the ambiguity of the applicable authoritative evidence and the resulting level of risk associated with the final decision.

JUDGMENT AND DECISION-MAKING RESEARCH FRAMEWORKS AND EVALUATION CRITERIA

Researchers performing JDM research generally are seeking to describe judgment and decision behavior, evaluate their quality, and develop and test theories of the underlying psychological processes which produce that behavior (Libby 1981; Ashton 1982). Accounting JDM research primarily has relied on a branch of psychology called behavioral decision theory which is rooted in cognitive psychology, economics, and statistics. Most of this extant accounting JDM research has focussed on auditors and has been couched in the auditing context. Spanning approximately twenty years, auditing JDM research progressed from simple qualitative analysis of behavior to complex modeling of the cognitive processes underlying audit JDM. In contrast, tax JDM research still is in its infancy.

Four theoretical frameworks underlie both audit and most other JDM studies. These same frameworks are evident in tax JDM research and they provide a useful way of categorizing the papers included in this review (see table 1). Researchers employing these frameworks can use a variety of criteria to evaluate the quality of the JDM process or the resultant judgments and decisions. In the remainder of this section, we will provide a discussion of these evaluation criteria and frameworks directed toward tax researchers having less than complete familiarity with JDM research. More detailed (but oriented to accounting researchers) descriptions of these frameworks underlying accounting and auditing JDM research can be found in Libby (1981), Ashton (1982), and Ashton and Ashton (1995).

JDM Evaluation Criteria

Three classes of criteria have been used to evaluate JDM inputs, processes (e.g., information search) and/or outputs (e.g., the judgment, the decision): (1) Conformance to a normative model and accuracy; (2) Surrogate measures of conformance to a normative model and accuracy; and (3) Conformance with a descriptive model. Each class is discussed below.

Conformance to a normative model and *accuracy* criteria are used to directly evaluate JDM quality. When using these criteria, the researcher compares observed JDM to an external standard. In the case of conformance to a normative model (e.g., Bayes' rule), the quality of JDM performance refers to the degree to which a JDM input, process or output (e.g., expected utility or money) is the same as that prescribed by a normative model (e.g., transitivity, irrelevance of identical outcomes, independence of utility and probability, choices made relative to model predictions) (see Ashton 1982).[7] Unfortunately, in many, if not most, accounting, auditing and tax studies, this criterion has not been used due to limitations such as the lack of a normative model or insufficient knowledge of the form of the appropriate utility functions.

Using the accuracy criterion, a JDM researcher would evaluate the quality of performance by comparing judgments or decisions to an outcome realization (e.g., stock price). Accounting, auditing or tax researchers generally have not relied on accuracy because in most of these task settings there is no unambiguous outcome realization. For

---

7. Conformance with a normative model is not always informative because optimality is conditional on a variety of variables, thus making it very situation- and person-specific (Waller 1995; Waller and Jiambalvo 1984).

TABLE 1. Experimental JDM Research on Tax Professionals.

JDM Framework		Tax JDM Phase					
		Learn About & Document Client's Tax & Business/Personal Context	Identify, Rank, & Document Preliminary Alternatives	Information Search	Evaluate Information	Revise, Rank & Choose Among Alternatives	Explain, Justify & Document Alternatives
Policy Capturing					Bain & Kilpatrick (1990) Chang & McCarty (1988) Chow et al. (1986)		
Probabilistic Judgment					Cloyd (1993)		
Heuristics & Biases	Hindsight/ Outcome				Helleloid (1988)		
	Framing				Newberry et al. (1993) Schisler (1994)	Duncan et al (1989) Sanders & Wyndelts (1989)	
	Belief Revision				Pei et al. (1990) Pei et al. (1992) Mayper et al. (1993) Helleloid (1989)		

TABLE 1, Continued. Experimental JDM Research on Tax Professionals .

JDM Framework		Tax JDM Phase					
		Learn About & Document Client's Tax & Business/Personal Context	Identify, Rank, & Document Preliminary Alternatives	Information Search	Evaluate Information	Revise, Rank & Choose Among Alternatives	Explain, Justify & Document Alternatives
Heuristics & Biases, continued	Confirmation Proneness				Johnson (1993)		
Cognition & Knowledge	Knowledge & Performance	Bonner et al. (1992) Bonner et al. (1994)				Kaplan et al. (1988)	
	Knowledge, Motivation, & Performance			Cloyd (1995a) Cloyd (1995b) Spilker (1995) Spilker & Prawitt (1995)			
	Reasoning Processes			Krawczyk et al. (1994)	Davis & Mason (1994) Marchant et al. (1991) Marchant et al. (1992) Marchant et al. (1993) Schadewald & Robinson (1993)		

example, if a subject were exposed to a set of authoritative evidence and asked to rate its level of authoritative support, neither he or she nor the researcher knows the "actual" degree of authoritative support provided by that evidence. A few tax JDM studies have used as a proxy for accuracy the consensus judgments or decisions of a panel of experts.

When reliance on conformance to a normative model or accuracy has not been feasible, researchers often have relied on surrogate quality measures. Four such measures frequently have been used to evaluate the quality of judgments and decisions. *Consensus* refers to between-judge agreement. It usually has been measured as the mean correlation between the judgments/decisions of each pair of subjects. *Stability* refers to within-judge agreement. That is, stability indicates the extent to which an individual makes consistent judgments or decisions over time when faced with the same uncertain situation. Stability generally has been calculated as the correlation between a single subject's responses to the same stimuli at different points in time. *Cue usage* refers to the weight afforded information cues when a judgment or decision is made. It has been measured by the statistical significance of a cue in a model such as regression analysis and/or by omega-squared (i.e., a statistical estimate of the proportion of variance explained in a regression or analysis of variance model by a particular cue or set of cues). *Self-insight* has been measured by the correlation between a subject's cue usage and that subject's importance rating of each cue. Such a correlation reveals how aware an individual is of the judgment policy he or she actually used. Higher consensus, stability, and self-insight generally would be considered to be suggestive of higher quality judgments or decisions.

Finally, JDM researchers often use *conformance with a descriptive model* as an evaluation criterion. The researcher's focus, in such cases, is on ascertaining whether an effect predicted by a descriptive model of an independent variable on a dependent variable has been realized. Three types of conformance can be investigated, corresponding to various types of descriptive models of JDM, by comparing an observed and a predicted: (1) output, when a descriptive model provides predictions about differences in the direction and/or magnitude of judgments and/or decisions; (2) input-output relationship, when a descriptive model provides predictions based on an as if (paramorphic) process; and (3) process, when a descriptive model provides predictions about the process used to formulate a judgment or make a decision. The linkage between any detected differences between a descriptive model's predictions and observed effects and performance quality, however, is ambiguous because what constitutes optimal or good performance frequently is not known (e.g., degree of authoritative support provided by some evidence, degree of aggressiveness of advice that should be offered).

JDM Frameworks

Four theoretical frameworks underlie extant tax JDM research: policy capturing, probabilistic judgment, heuristic and biases, and cognition and knowledge. In a *policy-capturing study*, the researcher is seeking to identify relevant information cues and build "as if" models which describe how they are combined to formulate a judgment or make a decision under conditions of uncertainty (See Appendix A). Such conditions clearly are present in many tax JDM settings. For example, tax professionals regularly face uncertainty about the amount of substantial authority provided by a set of evidence for a proposed tax treatment. In many of these settings, as noted earlier, the researcher is not able to evaluate the quality of the judgment or decision with respect to accuracy. Instead, policy-capturing researchers often have relied on surrogate quality measures, including consensus, stability, cue usage, and self-insight.

In *probabilistic-judgment studies*, researchers build statistical models of JDM under uncertainty. These studies have had a variety of foci, including subjective probability distributions, the conformance of judgments and decisions to the axioms of decision theory (e.g., transitivity), combination and revision of probabilities, and maximization of expected value/utility. Tax JDM studies focussing on these issues are important because most tax judgments and decisions are made under conditions of uncertainty and tax professionals try to maximize some objective function. For example, after conducting a search and evaluation of authoritative evidence, a tax professional explicitly or implicitly will formulate a (prior) probability distribution concerning the likelihood that the IRS will not challenge a proposed tax treatment; subsequently, additional relevant authoritative evidence becomes available and he or she will use that information to revise his or her prior probability distribution into a posterior distribution. In addition to those already discussed, probabilistic judgment studies have used several criteria to evaluate the quality of probabilistic judgments, including the coherence of subjective probability distributions, comparison of individuals' subjective probabilities with objective probabilities, and comparison of probability judgments to statistical models such as expected value/utility maximization and Bayes' rule (See Appendix B).

In *heuristics-and-biases studies*, researchers are concerned with the extent to which and the conditions under which individuals do *not* conform to normative models of judgment and decision behavior (Kahneman, Slovic, and Tversky 1982; Hogarth 1987). Due to time constraints, cognitive limitations relative to the task demands, complexity and/or volume of relevant information, and uncertainty about the evidence itself, an individual may not be able to use a maximizing JDM strategy. Rather, he or she may use simplifying strategies (i.e., heuristics) which produce satisfactory results rather than optimal results. A consequence of such simplifications, however, is that judgments and decisions may be "biased" because they deviate from solutions prescribed by the use of normative models. JDM studies have been reported in which tax professionals' usage of four heuristic processes and resultant biases were investigated—framing effects, hindsight/outcome effects, belief adjustment, and confirmation proneness. A description of each heuristic is presented in Appendix C, along with a discussion of the associated studies.

In *cognition and knowledge studies*, researchers attempt to elucidate the cognitive processes used to transform information in the environment and information already in long-term memory into judgments and decisions. Studies based on other JDM frameworks use *as if* assumptions or models (e.g., algebraic formulas) to map the transformation of information in the environment to judgments and decisions. In contrast, cognition and knowledge studies are either explicitly or implicitly based on models of memory structure and processes which recognize that the person formulating the judgment or making the decision will encode, store, recall and transform information. For example, analogical reasoning and similarity judgments have been the focus of tax JDM research (see Appendix D). Many of these studies examine various linkages among judgment and decision performance and their determinants: ability, experience, knowledge, and motivation/incentives (Libby and Luft 1993).

REVIEW OF RESEARCH ON TAX PROFESSIONALS' JUDGMENT AND DECISION MAKING

The scope of our literature review is restricted to 27 published and working-paper studies in which researchers report experimental tests of hypotheses derived from at least one of the four JDM frameworks described earlier[8] *and* the subjects are tax professionals[9] working in public accounting firms. Research focussed on JDM of both taxpayers and tax regulators, such as revenue agents employed by the IRS, are excluded from this review. Very few studies have focussed on tax regulators, making a systematic review and analysis of that literature of limited value.[10] In contrast, a critical mass of studies now have been reported in which taxpayers' behavior was investigated from a variety of perspectives (including JDM, but also including social psychology as well as economics and sociology). We excluded all of these studies because of a desire to focus on tax professionals' JDM which, as observed earlier, is both important in practice and recently has received considerable research attention. We also have excluded research which is focussed on tax judgments and decisions that occur during interactions (e.g., negotiations, bargaining) among tax professionals, taxpayers and tax regulators since much of this research is couched in game theoretic terms, rather than relying on theories of JDM. Related, no studies focusing on multiperson information processing are included.[11] Finally, our review is restricted to studies in which experiments were used to test hypotheses.[12] We define an experiment as the manipulation of independent variables, measurement of that effect on the dependent variables, and the use of inferential statistics to ascertain whether the observed effect is or is not due to chance.

Each of these 27 tax studies is summarized in Appendices A–D.[13] In the remainder of this section, we describe prominent features of the

8. The decision concerning whether a study falls within the boundaries of a particular JDM framework involves subjectivity. As one example, Cuccia (1994) provides an experimental test of whether tax professionals' judgments are affected by certain behavioral and economic variables. The latter variables are modeled from an agency-incentive perspective which, in some ways, can be similar to that of probabilistic judgment studies. We did, however, exclude this paper from our review because the analysis therein is not directly consistent with any of the four JDM frameworks.

9. Our literature search identified studies with three types of student subjects. First, those studies in which the student subjects were not explicitly identified as having had professional tax experience were excluded from our study. Second, those studies in which the student subjects were identified as having had professional tax experience were included. Third, studies were included when the student subjects were enrolled in a master of tax program and their purpose was to provide a baseline against which to compare tax professionals' knowledge or experience.

10. We are aware of no studies in which tax regulators or members of the judiciary were the subjects. There, however, are a few studies in which an empirical modeling approach, somewhat like policy capturing, was used to *ex post* model the decisions of judges and courts (e.g., Robison (1983)).

11. We identified only one such study (Carnes, Harwood, and Sawyers 1993).

12. Three studies included in our review met all of the inclusion criteria except this one. They have been included, however, because they provide a point of departure to several important issues.

"typical" tax JDM study, thereby establishing a bridge to the critical commentary in the next section.

Description of the Representative Study

The description below is intended to provide a reader who is not familiar with the experimental studies in which tax professionals' JDM has been investigated with a general understanding of the focus and features of a typical study. While no single study has all of the features described below, our caricature provides a useful bridge to the critical discussion in the next section.

In the typical study—63% of the studies—the researcher focussed on the information evaluation phase (table 1). Further, in almost all of the studies, the tax professional-subject faced a closed-fact situation. The subject also was in a passive mode since the information he or she was asked to evaluate was provided by the researcher and he or she was asked to respond, using a predetermined-response scale, to an average of three questions (dependent variables). The tax professional-subjects typically had about five years of experience working for a national public accounting firm.

About 45 types of dependent variables were employed in the tax JDM studies we have reviewed, 35 of which were used in a single study. The three most frequently used dependent variables were a recommendation to the client concerning how aggressive he or she should be about deducting an expense (14%), the degree of authoritative support provided by a particular set of information (13%), and a prediction of the success of a tax treatment in court (8%). In terms of JDM evaluation criteria, 81% of the dependent variables were conformance with a descriptive model, eight percent were accuracy/maximization, and 11% were surrogate measures of accuracy. Few studies used multiple measures of a dependent variable.

The researcher typically developed directional hypotheses based on a direct transfer of extant psychology theory and one of the JDM frameworks to the tax context. Across all of the studies, 49% of the substantive hypotheses concerned the individual (i.e., the tax professional), 43% the task,[14] and eight percent the individual-by-task interaction. In many studies, there was a somewhat loose connection

13. We apologize to authors whose published or unpublished studies were inadvertently omitted.

14. This 43% is comprised of three types of task-related variables: evidential (25%), the client (11%), the situation (6%), and interactions between task variables (1%).

among the psychology literature reviewed, the hypotheses, the design of the experiment, and tests of the hypotheses. For example, independent variables often have been included in an experiment even though they did not directly follow from the particular JDM framework underlying the study.[15] Rather, some independent variables appear to have been included in the experiment because they are present in the natural ecology. Usually, however, there were no theory-based hypotheses provided which articulated the cognitive mechanism by which such variables were expected to affect the dependent variables.

Across all of the studies, 46% of the independent variables related to characteristics of the tax professional (e.g., experience, tax knowledge). The remaining independent variables related to the task, specifically evidential characteristics (e.g., order of evidence, outcome) (25%), client characteristics (e.g., risk attitude, withholding position) (15%), and situational characteristics (e.g., IRS audit probability) (14%). Fifty-six percent of the independent variables were manipulated (88% between subject and 12% within subject) and the remaining 44% were measured (e.g., experience). Of the manipulated variables, there was a manipulation check reported for only 35%. Finally, the results section in many studies provided a minimum level of disclosure of descriptive and inferential statistics such that there was some difficulty in understanding whether or not the hypotheses were rejected.

A CRITICAL ANALYSIS OF RESEARCH ON TAX PROFESSIONALS' JUDGMENT AND DECISION MAKING

Several observations follow from an analysis of the extant tax JDM literature. For example, it is noteworthy that the focus of the typical tax JDM study has shifted rather quickly (e.g., relative to a similar evolution in auditing JDM studies) from simply investigating inputs and outputs (i.e., policy capturing, probabilistic judgment) and ways in which tax professionals might violate psychological and economic norms (i.e., heuristic and biases) to examination of the cognitive processing by which prior knowledge and information in the environment is accessed to support judgment formulation and decision-making (i.e., cognition, knowledge).

We believe that the extant studies have enhanced in important respects our understanding of how and how well tax professionals formulate judgments and make decisions. For example, light has been

---

15. Across all of the studies, 32% of the independent variables were not directly included in hypotheses.

shed on the extent of between-tax professional agreement/disagreement in "substantial authority" judgments by the extant policy-capturing studies and on the descriptive validity of prospect theory versus subjective expected utility for various phases of tax JDM. Our understanding has been increased with regard to the extent to which tax professionals use simplifying rules-of-thumb (and their consequences) when selecting tax treatments to recommend to a client in a closed-fact situation. In open-fact situations, the linkage between specialized tax knowledge and performance has begun to be elucidated by cognition and knowledge studies.

Extant JDM tax research also has contributed by providing evidence relevant to revision of generic theories of JDM. For example, it has been reported by Newberry, Reckers, and Wyndelts (1993) that the reflection effect of prospect theory is stronger when the attendant JDM consequences directly accrue to the experimental subject relative to when they only indirectly are germane to the experimental subject. Clearly, tax JDM research has come a long way in a short time. It now, however, would seem prudent to consider ways in which the payoffs from the scarce resources which are expended in the conduct of tax JDM can be further enhanced. We offer the ensuing critical analysis in that spirit.

JDM Phases and Activities

We will begin by referring to table 1 and observing that only rather limited aspects of tax JDM tasks have been investigated to date. Notice that numerous cells have few or no entries. One might argue that the dispersion of studies indicates the relative importance of different tasks and research frameworks. We do not believe, however, that such an argument is sustainable. For example, there are no studies in any of the cells comprising the "Explain, Justify and Document Alternatives and Choice" and "Identify, Rank and Document Preliminary Alternatives" columns, despite the obvious importance of these phases of tax JDM.[16]

Most of the studies reported to date focus on certain categories of cognitive activities to the exclusion of other such activities. As noted earlier, *construction processes* expand the set of information available for JDM (e.g., they involve generation of ideas and interpretations) while *reduction processes* are directed at information set compression (Bonner and Pennington 1991). For both open- and closed-fact situations, construction processes play a critical role, particularly in the early phases

16. This shortcoming also is shared by audit JDM studies (Solomon and Shields 1995).

of the JDM process. The overwhelming majority of the existing tax JDM studies, however, focussed on reduction processes.[17] Further, in most existing tax JDM research, the subjects have been asked to perform a closed-fact task. Indeed, with only a few exceptions, the extant research has focussed on reduction cognitive processes in a closed-fact situation. Even a cursory review of tax textbooks or informal discussions with tax professionals, however, reveals that the most intriguing, difficult and profitable tasks performed by expert/experienced tax professionals relate to the planning and constructive part of tax JDM.

Recognizing that good problem structuring is a key to successful problem solving, there also has been a call in non-tax JDM research to focus on the front-end of problem solving (von Winterfeldt and Edwards 1986). We believe that this call is on target and that a recently developed framework provides especially useful perspectives for the tax setting. Keller and Ho (1989) have proposed a framework of methods used to generate alternatives for ill-defined problem-solving tasks. They argue, for example, that alternative generation involves a search through the individual's cognitive network (i.e., memory) and, therefore, any research on alternative generation must be based on a valid description of the way the individual's knowledge is stored in and accessed from long-term memory. In that regard, the Bonner, Davis, and Jackson (1994) study represents a necessary first step in the investigation of constructive processes of tax professionals.

Research examining the constructive processes of tax professionals might benefit from the psychological research on divergent thinking and creative performance in problem solving. Divergent thinking involves the production of varied responses to a problem or a question that has multiple alternative solutions (Runco 1991) while creative performance in problem solving involves the production of solutions which are novel, clever, and/or innovative (Barron 1988). Importantly, several models of creative performance in tasks such as divergent thinking have been proposed in the psychology literature. One model proposes five categories of variables which may have independent and interactive effects on performance (Isaksen, Puccio, Treffinger 1993). These categories of variables are personal orientation, situational outlook, task characteristics, the problem-solving process, and outcome. The tax accounting environment provides a broad range of these factors which could be difficult to capture in a generic, laboratory decision-making task. Thus, tax researchers are in a good position to

---

17. This observation also is true for auditing JDM research and is probably due to the ease of generating hypotheses and designing experiments to investigate reduction processes relative to constructive processes (Bonner and Pennington 1991).

contribute to the creative performance literature with regard to the independent and interactive effects of such factors.

Theory Construction and Testing

In this subsection, we will discuss two critical aspects of theory construction and testing. First is the selection of theoretic variables and a continuum of possibilities exists. At one extreme, the JDM researcher could survey the natural ecology of the targeted (tax) JDM task environment and include only those variables thought to be important. At the other extreme, the researcher could select variables based on generic (psychology) theory (i.e., without reference to the natural ecology of the (tax) environment).

Second is the number, type and connectedness of the relationships among the theoretic variables. For example, one could model or predict and test tax JDM behavior in a piecemeal fashion, by focussing on a set of relatively disconnected bivariate, linear relationships for a small subset of theoretic variables. Alternatively, one could focus on a relatively complete system of variables for which the underlying logic stems from a particular theoretic perspective (e.g., maximization of expected utility). Importantly, the type of interrelationships may be linear or more complex (e.g., nonlinear, interactive).

Our view is that a most profitable research strategy is to select complementary variables from both the natural tax ecology and (psychology) theories because of their significance to successful performance on the tax task or issue being studied and then investigate multiple types of interrelationships among the variables. Davis and Mason (1994) is an example of research in which the variables were selected from both the natural tax ecology and psychology theory. These authors investigated tax professionals' evaluation of authoritative support using a psychology model of similarity judgment. However, they modified the psychology model by incorporating variables from the natural tax ecology (e.g., client advocacy). The development of a "tailored" model is facilitated by focussing on a system of (linear, nonlinear, interactive, multivariate) interrelationships among the variables. An example of research which investigates the interrelationships among a system of variables is Cloyd (1995a). In his examination of tax professionals' information search, he used the "expertise" paradigm (Libby and Luft 1993) to develop and test hypotheses not only about the main effects (i.e., bivariate, linear relationships) of knowledge and incentives on performance, but also their interactive effects.

Our analysis of the extant tax JDM studies indicates that, when selecting variables, researchers have sampled both the natural ecology and the generic psychology theory. Such sampling, however, has not necessarily resulted in the selection of the most performance-dependent variables and there has been insufficient attention paid to the interconnectedness among the variable interrelationships. Several deleterious consequences follow.

Importantly, when independent variables are selected from the natural ecology but little or no causal theory is developed ex ante to explain how the independent variables affect the dependent variables, there inevitably will be a diminished ability to make causal attributions (i.e., to explain how some or all of the independent variables affect the dependent variables). This problem is most evident in several studies we reviewed in which independent variables were included without any related hypotheses. Similarly, many of the studies we reviewed relied on psychology theories for selection of variables without adapting such theories in light of important features of the tax environment. If the tax scholar had exploited his or her comparative advantage as an applied researcher and focussed on developing a theory of the tax task, the hypotheses and results are likely to have been more informative (See the discussion of the role of pre-experimental research that follows). Although in-depth knowledge of tax content and structural features is a comparative advantage of the tax JDM researcher, generally such knowledge has been insufficiently exploited to date by tax JDM researchers. Learning opportunities with respect to generic psychology theory and the behavior of tax professionals have been adversely affected.

For example, Helleloid (1988) reported that his subjects did not exhibit non-normative use of outcome information. This result is in contrast to the results reported by a substantial number of JDM studies in a variety of other settings and, thus it is potentially important. Pei, Reckers, and Wyndelts (1992) observed an interesting relationship between experience and order effects—more experienced tax professionals exhibited greater order effects. Further, Helleloid (1989) reported another interesting experience effect—a non-monotonic relationship between tax professionals' experience and their aggressiveness. Still another example is the study on similarity judgment by Schadewald and Robinson (1993) that reported results which were inconsistent with their psychology-based predictions, yet it is difficult to isolate why. Specifically, we are unable to identify whether the unpredicted results are due to inappropriate transfer of theory, theoretic misspecification of the task, tax task content or context omissions or commissions, or subject-related characteristics (e.g., lack of necessary knowledge, incentive to process information).

Finally, the lack of connectedness among the variable interrelationships has resulted in an overwhelming majority (92%) of the hypotheses being concerned with the main effects of individual or task characteristics while only 8% of substantive hypotheses have addressed individual-by-task interactions. This preponderance of main-effect hypotheses conflicts with much non-tax JDM research in which behavior increasingly is modeled as a function of the processor-by-task interaction (Einhorn and Hogarth 1981; Payne, Bettman and Johnson 1993; Solomon and Shields 1995). Thus, an important way in which tax researchers can improve tax JDM research would be to exploit their institutional knowledge by performing more in-depth theoretical and empirical analyses of how characteristics of the tax professional (e.g., risk preference, knowledge) interact with characteristics of a tax task (e.g., audit probability, degree of authoritative support) to determine the tax professional's behavior (e.g., problem identification, construction of alternatives).

Multiperson and Multiperiod Issues

We believe that important variables that should be included in research to expand the scope of tax JDM theories relate to the multiperson and multiperiod nature of tax JDM. As previously discussed, the tax professional seeks to protect and enhance his or her professional reputation with the IRS and other regulatory and judicial agencies, his or her current and prospective clients, his or her public accounting colleagues (e.g., the review process, promotions) as well as the public accounting profession. Related to reputation management, the tax professional is accountable to these parties and, therefore, must document, justify, and defend his or her judgments and decisions. The future period consequences associated with reputation management, justification, and defensibility sometimes are so great that we believe they can be primary objectives of the tax professional. As such, it would seem that they should be a major focus of tax JDM research. A primary focus of such research would be investigating how tax professionals construct and document a case to make it defensible. Cloyd (1995a) is the only study in which an experiment was designed to provide an examination of the subjects' documentation process (i.e., the subjects constructed notebooks of the evidence judged to be relevant).

The Role of Pre-Experimental JDM Tax Research

An important priority, as we discussed earlier, is to conduct descriptive research aimed at providing a deeper and broader understanding of the natural ecology of the environments in which tax JDM occurs. This requires tax JDM researchers to engage in two types of pre-experimental research. One type is field research, which involves identifying and descriptively modeling the important JDM tax issues and their associated antecedent and consequence variables. For example, we believe that such research would find that issues related to the documentation of a client's case and how and how well defensibility judgments are formulated for open-fact tasks are very important. Second, based on this descriptive research, tax JDM researchers should conduct intensive task analyses of the important judgments and decisions previously identified. Below is a more detailed discussion of the importance of, and issues involved with, these two types of research.

One potentially profitable focus of tax JDM research is identifying and describing what expert tax professionals consider to be important tax judgments and decisions and the factors that influence their JDM process. Such descriptive research would be important to ensure that tax JDM research is focussed on significant aspects of, and problems related to, tax practice, in contrast to having tax JDM research focus on that which is of more concern in the non-tax JDM research literature. For this research to be most valuable, it probably should be approached using an open, inductive style. Further, if this descriptive research were to lead to lists of observations which subsequently are classified into taxonomies so that regularities are highlighted, another contribution would have been made. Field or case studies may be particularly useful for these purposes. It also may be most productive to focus initially on a relatively few tax experts who are believed to be able to provide deep and broad descriptions of tax practice. Subsequently, to substantiate and extend these studies, one might consider using open- and closed-ended surveys with various degrees of structuredness. To provide a guide for such descriptive research, tax JDM researchers can refer to the auditing studies by Gibbins and Wolf (1982), Emby and Gibbins (1988), Gibbins (1988), Gibbins and Newton (1994), and Hirst and Koonce (1994). Milliron's (1988) investigation of factors that influence tax professionals' aggressiveness is an example of a descriptive field study approach.

After performing descriptive research, task analysis can be used to increase knowledge about the important tax judgments and decisions by formalizing and extending the available descriptive models. Task analysis, which is rooted in disciplines such as psychology, computer science, statistics, law, economics, and operations research, may be used to causally model the processes and information used to move from an initial state (e.g., request by a client for a recommended tax treatment) to a goal state (e.g., choice of recommended tax treatment). A key outcome of task analysis is testable hypotheses. Peters (1993) provides a discussion of the importance of, and how to conduct, task analysis research in accounting and auditing. Bonner and Pennington (1991) and Bonner (1994) provide task analyses of many audit judgment and decisions that can serve as a model for tax JDM researchers. Conducting a task analysis that is based on descriptive models and practice literature (e.g., firms' training and policy manuals) helps to ensure that theories and research methods transferred from other disciplines are appropriate to the tax JDM issue at hand (Solomon and Shields 1995).

Experimental Method Issues

With our final set of critical comments, we discuss methodological ways to improve experimental tax JDM research. The quality and reliability of tax JDM research could be improved if researchers attended to three measurement issues. First, using multiple measures of measured variables could increase their reliability. For example, in one of the few studies to include multiple measures, Cloyd (1995b) used a total of 20 measures of three types of information search behavior. Second, we observed that the hypotheses in several studies depended on subjects' risk preferences, yet generally, there only was weak measurement and/or control of risk preference. Third, a shift in tax JDM research to a focus on defensibility raises interesting measurement issues. Specifically, when documentation, justification and/or defensibility quality are the dependent variables, ways to measure such variables and capture differences in the JDM performance evaluation criteria (e.g., maximization, accuracy, consensus) need to be developed. In many cases, the researcher might rely on a panel of experts either to provide a benchmark solution to assess the quality of judgments or to "grade" the subjects' judgments in justifiability/defensibility terms. In contrast, when used as independent variables, innovative operationalization must be developed so that the variables are calibrated to the hypotheses being tested.

In addition, in these studies, JDM performance usually was assessed with respect to conformance with a descriptive model. This emphasis reflects the researcher's interest in testing for differences in dependent variables caused by manipulation of the independent variables. Importantly, however, only limited information about JDM quality can be provided when such variables are extensively used. Coupling difference dependent variables with assessments of maximization/accuracy can greatly enhance what is learned about tax professionals' JDM.

Several other opportunities exist to improve experimental tax JDM research. For example, the inclusion of manipulation checks would help discern why statistically insignificant results may have been obtained (e.g., were weak manipulations of independent variables responsible?). The completeness of descriptive and inferential statistics reported in a paper could be increased. While we are in favor of parsimony, greater disclosure, in many instances, would have greatly improved our understanding of the results of the hypothesis testing.

Finally, three of the tax JDM studies included in Table 2 raise an interesting method issue. The authors of these three studies (Bonner et al. 1992, 1994; Cloyd 1995b) did not manipulate any independent variables, thus, strictly speaking, they are not true experiments but quasi-experiments. One reason that independent variables were not manipulated in these studies was the authors' focus on identifying the effects of knowledge on information search behavior or judgment performance. It would be very costly for researchers to manipulate knowledge by first establishing pre-experiment equivalence among all subjects, for example, on their level of knowledge and then randomly assign them to treatment conditions in which each treatment would be exposed to a different amount and/or type of knowledge (e.g., in the extreme, this approach could require several semesters of education and, possibly, some practice experience).

Instead, a researcher may be forced to acquire a sample of subjects who are believed to have variation in their knowledge (e.g., students vs. tax partners) and then to measure their knowledge. Under this approach, the researcher does not incur the cost of manipulating knowledge but the benefits lost include the ability to test causality (e.g., that variation in knowledge caused the detected differences in JDM). The lack of random assignment of subjects who have (assumed) pre-experimental equivalence on different levels of the independent variable severely reduces the researcher's ability to demonstrate that other variables did not cause any observed effect on the dependent variable. To compensate for this loss in ability to infer causality, researchers should identify, at a minimum, the most likely competing explanations, and include multiple measures of each independent variable associated with each explanation to try to statistically eliminate these competing explanations.

CONCLUDING REMARKS

It is our hope that we have successfully communicated two macro themes with respect to the growing literature on tax professionals' JDM. In our view, much has been accomplished in a short time period. Noteworthy is that only 27 papers meet our criteria for inclusion and one third of them are unpublished working papers. However, while there has been considerable progress, numerous opportunities exist for enhancing the value of future research on tax professionals' JDM.

Some of these opportunities involve changing the foci researchers might adopt when planning and executing future studies and making greater usage of the researchers' knowledge of tax content, tax structural features, the tax professional, and the interaction amongst them. Other important research opportunities include experimental design and other method-based improvements, especially those that allow the researcher to more definitively link findings to theory, thereby enhancing what we can learn both about tax professional's JDM and human behavior in general.

ACKNOWLEDGMENTS

We appreciate the comments provided on an earlier draft of this paper by Urton Anderson, Stan Biggs, Bryan Cloyd, Jon Davis, Jackie Hammersley, Kathryn Kadous, Anne Magro, Gary Marchant, Jim Peters, Jay Rich and John Robinson.

REFERENCES

Abelson, R. 1981. The psychological status of the script concept. *American Psychologist* 36: 715–729.

Ashton, R. 1982. *Human Information Processing in Accounting, Studies in Accounting Research #17*. Sarasota, FL: American Accounting Association.

Ashton, R., and A. Ashton, eds. 1995. *Judgment and Decision Research in Accounting and Auditing*. New York, NY: Cambridge University Press.

Bain C., and B. Kilpatrick. 1990. A note on professionals' judgments of tax authority. *The Journal of the American Taxation Association* (Fall): 78–87.

Barron, F. 1988. Putting creativity to work. In *The Nature of Creativity*, edited by R. Sternberg. New York, NY: Cambridge University Press.

Bonner, S. 1994. A model of the effects of audit task complexity. *Accounting, Organizations and Society* 19 (3): 213–234.

Bonner, S., J. Davis, and B. Jackson. 1992. Expertise in corporate tax planning: The issue identification stage. *Journal of Accounting Research* 30 (Supplement): 1–28.

Bonner, S., J. Davis, and B. Jackson. 1994. Expertise-related differences in the organization of knowledge used for corporate tax issue identification. Working paper, University of Southern California.

Bonner, S., and N. Pennington. 1991. Cognitive processes and knowledge as determinants of auditor expertise. *Journal of Accounting Literature* 10: 1–50.

Brown, C., and I. Solomon. 1993. An experimental investigation of explanations for outcome effects on appraisals of capital budgeting decisions. *Contemporary Accounting Research* (Fall): 82–111.

Carnes, G., G. Harwood, and R. Sawyers. 1993. A comparison of tax professionals' individual and group decisions when resolving ambiguous tax questions. Working paper, Georgia State University.

Chang, O., and T. McCarty. 1988. Evidence on judgment involving the determination of substantial authority: Tax practitioners versus students. *The Journal of the American Taxation Association* (Fall): 26–39.

Chow, C., M. Shields, and G. Whittenburg. 1989. The quality of practitioners' judgments regarding substantial authority: An exploratory empirical investigation. *Advances in Taxation* 2: 165–180.

Cloyd, C. 1993. The effects of financial accounting conformity and on recommendations of tax preparers. Working paper, The University of Texas at Austin.

Cloyd, C. 1995a. Performance in tax research tasks: The joint effects of knowledge and accountability. Working paper, The University of Texas at Austin.

Cloyd, C. 1995b. Prior knowledge, information search behaviors, and performance in tax research tasks. *Journal of the American Tax Association* (forthcoming).

Cuccia, A., 1994. The effects of increased sanctions on paid tax preparers: Integrating economic and psychological factors. *The Journal of the American Tax Association* 16 (Spring): 41–66.

Davis, J., and J. Mason. 1995. The role of similarity in tax authority judgments. Working paper, University of Illinois at Urbana–Champaign.

Duncan, W., D. LaRue, and P. Reckers. 1989. An empirical examination of the influence of selected economic and noneconomic variables on decision-making by tax professionals. *Advances in Taxation* 2: 91–106.

Einhorn, H. 1974. Expert judgment: Some necessary conditions and an example. *Journal of Applied Psychology* 59 (5): 562–571.

Einhorn, H., and R. Hogarth. 1981. Behavioral decision theory: Processes of judgment and choice. *Annual Review of Psychology*: 53–88.

Einhorn, H., and R. Hogarth. 1985. Ambiguity and uncertainty in probabilistic inference. *Psychological Review* (October): 433–461.

Emby, C., and M. Gibbins. 1988. Good judgment in public accounting: Quality and justification. *Contemporary Accounting Research* (Spring): 287–313.

Fischer, C., M. Wartick, and M. Mark. 1992. Detection probability and taxpayer compliance: A review of the literature. *Journal of Accounting Literature* 11: 1–46.

Gentner, D. 1982. Are scientific analogies metaphors? In *Metaphor: Problems and Perspectives*, edited by D. Miall, 106–132. Brighton, Sussex: Harvester Press.

Gibbins, M. 1988. Knowledge structures and experienced auditor judgment. In *Auditor Productivity in the Year 2000: 1987 Proceedings of the Eleventh Arthur Young Professors' Roundtable*, edited by A. Bailey, 51–82. Reston Virginia: Council of Arthur Young Professors.

Gibbins, M., and K. Jamal. 1993. Problem-centered research and knowledge-based theory in the professional accounting setting. *Accounting, Organizations and Society* 18 (5): 451–466.

Gibbins, M., and J. Newton. 1994. An empirical exploration of complex accountability in public accounting. *Journal of Accounting Research* 32 (Fall): 165–186.

Gibbins, M., and F. Wolf. 1982. Auditor's subjective decision environment—The case of a normal external audit. *The Accounting Review* (January): 105–124.

Helleloid, R. 1988. Hindsight judgments about taxpayers' expectations. *The Journal of the American Taxation Association* (Spring): 31–46.

Helleloid, R. 1989. Ambiguity and the evaluation of client documentation by tax professionals. *The Journal of the American Taxation Association* (Fall): 22–36.

Hirst, D., and L. Koonce. 1994. Audit analytical procedures: A field investigation. Working paper, University of Texas at Austin.

Hogarth, R. 1987. *Judgment and Choice*, Second edition. New York, NY: John Wiley & Sons.

Hogarth, R., and H. Einhorn. 1992. Order effects in belief updating: The belief-adjustment model. *Cognitive Psychology* (January): 1–55.

Internal Revenue Service. 1987. Tables 13 and 14 of statistical series. *Statistics of Income Bulletin* (Spring).

Isaksen, S., G. Puccio, and D. Treffinger. 1993. An ecological approach to creativity research: Profiling for creative problem solving. *Journal of Creative Behavior* 27(3): 149–170.

Jackson, B., and V. Milliron. 1986. Tax compliance research: Findings, problems, and prospects. *Journal of Accounting Literature* 5: 125–165.

Johnson, L. 1993. An empirical investigation of the effects of advocacy on preparers' evaluations of judicial evidence. *The Journal of the American Taxation Association* (Spring): 1–22.

Johnson-Laird, P. 1983. *Mental Models*. Cambridge, MA: Harvard University Press.

Kahneman, D., P. Slovic, and A. Tversky, eds. 1982. *Judgment Under Uncertainty: Heuristics and Biases*. Cambridge, England: Cambridge University Press.

Kahneman, D., and A. Tversky. 1979. Prospect theory: An analysis of decision under risk. *Econometrica* (March): 263–291.

Kaplan, S., P. Reckers, S. West, and J. Boyd. 1988. An examination of tax reporting recommendations of professional tax preparers. *Journal of Economic Psychology* 9: 427–443.

Keller, L., and J. Ho. 1989. Decision problem structuring: Generating options. *IEEE Transactions on Systems, Man, and Cybernetics* (September/October): 715–728.

Klayman, J., and Y. Ha. 1987. Confirmation, disconfirmation, and information in hypothesis testing. *Psychological Review* 94(2): 211–228.

Klayman, J., and Y. Ha. 1989. Hypothesis testing in rule discovery: Strategy, structure, and content. *Journal of Experimental Psychology: Learning, Memory, and Cognition* 15(4): 596–604.

Krawczyk, K., G. Marchant, and J. Robinson. 1994. Constraint satisfaction in the selection of tax authorities. Working paper, North Carolina State University.

Libby, R. 1981. *Accounting and Human Information Processing: Theory and Applications*. Englewood Cliffs, NJ: Prentice–Hall, Inc.

Libby, R., and J. Luft. 1993. Determinants of judgment performance in accounting settings: Ability, knowledge, motivation and environment. *Accounting, Organizations and Society* 18(5): 425–450.

Magro, A. 1995. Contextual effects in tax research: An experimental investigation of adaptivity and performance in an information search task. Dissertation proposal, University of Illinois at Urbana–Champaign.

Marchant, G., J. Robinson, U. Anderson, and M. Schadewald. 1989. A cognitive model of tax problem solving. *Advances in Taxation* 2: 1–20.

Marchant, G., J. Robinson, U. Anderson, and M. Schadewald. 1991. Analogical transfer and expertise in legal reasoning. *Organizational Behavior and Human Decision Processes* 48: 272–290.

Marchant, G., J. Robinson, U. Anderson, and M. Schadewald. 1992. Analogy and tax problem solving. *Advances in Taxation* 4: 225–246.

Marchant, G., J. Robinson, U. Anderson, and M. Schadewald. 1993. The use of analogy in legal argument: Problem similarity, precedent, and expertise. *Organizational Behavior and Human Decision Processes* 55: 95–119.

Mayer, R. 1992. *Thinking, Problem Solving, Cognition*, Second Edition. New York: W.H. Freeman and Company.

Mayper, A., B. Kilpatrick, and U. Anderson. 1993. Tax workpaper review: An examination of the effects of order and conclusion presentation. Working paper, University of North Texas.

Milliron, V. 1988. A conceptual model of factors influencing tax preparers' aggressiveness. In *Contemporary Tax Research,* edited by S. Moriarity and J. Collins. Norman, OK: The Center for Economic and Management Research, University of Oklahoma.

Minsky, M. 1975. A framework for representing knowledge. In *The Psychology of Computer Vision,* edited by P.H. Winston. New York, NY: McGraw–Hill.

Newberry, K., P. Reckers, and R. Wyndelts. 1993. An examination of tax practitioner decisions: The role of preparer sanctions and framing effects associated with client condition. *Journal of Economic Psychology* 14: 439–452.

Norwood, F., S. Chisholm, F. Burke, Jr., and D. Vaughan. 1979. *Federal Taxation: Research, Planning and Procedures,* Second Edition. Englewood Cliffs, NJ: Prentice–Hall, Inc.

Payne, J., J. Bettman, and E. Johnson. 1993. *The Adaptive Decision Maker.* New York, NY: Cambridge University Press.

Pei, B., P. Reckers, and R. Wyndelts. 1990. The influence of information presentation order on professional tax judgment. *Journal of Economic Psychology* 11: 119–146.

Pei, B., P. Reckers, and R. Wyndelts. 1992. Tax professionals' belief revision: The effects of information presentation sequence, client preference, and domain experience. *Decision Sciences* 23: 175–199.

Peters, J. 1993. Decision-making, cognitive science and accounting: An overview of the intersection. *Accounting, Organizations and Society* 18 (July): 383–405.

Raabe, W., G. Whittenburg, and J. Bost. 1993. *West's Federal Tax Research,* Third Edition. New York, NY: West Publishing Co.

Robison, J. 1983. Tax court classification of activities not engaged in for profit: Some empirical evidence. *The Journal of the American Tax Association* (Fall): 7–22.

Ross, L. 1977. The intuitive psychologist and his shortcomings: Distortions in the attribution process. In *Advances in Experimental Social Psychology* 10, edited by L. Berkowitz. New York, NY: Academic Press, Inc.

Runco, M. 1991. *Divergent Thinking.* Norwood, NJ: Ablex.

Sanders, D., and R. Wyndelts. 1989. An examination of tax practitioners' decisions under uncertainty. *Advances in Taxation* 2: 41–72.

Schadewald, M., and J. Robinson. 1993. Similarity judgments of accounting professionals: How generalizable is Tversky's (1977) diagnosticity hypothesis? Working paper, University of Wisconsin–Milwaukee.

Schank, R., and R. Abelson. 1977. *Scripts, Plans, Goals, and Understanding: An Inquiry into Human Knowledge Structures.* Hillsdale, NJ: Lawrence Erlbaum.

Schisler, D. 1994. An experimental examination of factors affecting tax preparers' aggressiveness—a prospect theory approach. *The Journal of the American Tax Association* (Fall): 124–142.

Scholes, M., and M. Wolfson. 1992. *Taxes and Business Strategy: A Planning Approach*. Englewood Cliffs, NJ: Prentice–Hall, Inc.

Solomon, I., and M. Shields. 1995. Judgment and decision research in auditing. In *Judgment and Decision Research in Accounting and Auditing*, edited by R. Ashton and A. Ashton. New York, NY: Cambridge University Press.

Sommerfeld, R., and G. Streuling. 1981 *Tax Research Techniques*, Second Edition. New York, NY: American Institute of Certified Public Accountants.

Spilker, B. 1995. The effects of time pressure and knowledge on key word selection behavior in tax research. *The Accounting Review* 70 (January): 49–70.

Spilker, B., and D. Prawitt. 1995. Adaptive responses to time pressure: The effects of experience on tax information search behavior. Working paper, Brigham Young University.

Tversky, A. 1977. Features of similarity. *Psychological Review* 84 (July): 327–352.

von Winterfelt, D., and W. Edwards. 1986. *Decision Analysis and Behavioral Research*. New York, NY: Cambridge University Press.

Waller, W. 1995. Decision research in managerial accounting: Return to behavioral economics foundations. In *Judgment and Decision-making Research in Accounting and Auditing*, edited by R. Ashton and A. Ashton. New York, NY: Cambridge University Press.

Waller, W., and J. Jiambalvo. 1984. The use of normative models in human information processing research in accounting. *Journal of Accounting Literature* 3:201–226.

APPENDIX A: POLICY-CAPTURING STUDIES

Policy-capturing methods were employed in three studies to examine tax professionals' substantial-authority judgments. As noted in the text, tax professionals in both open- and closed-fact situations often face the task of determining the strength of authoritative evidence (also referred to as determination of substantial authority). However, no explicit guidelines have been established by law for weighting conflicting sources of authoritative evidence. A tax professional, therefore, must rely upon his or her "professional judgment" in evaluating authority. Because there is no external referent for appraising these judgments, judgment consensus, judgment consistency, and self-insight into cue usage have been used in the three studies to describe and evaluate JDM performance. These studies, therefore, have relied on the notion developed by Einhorn (1974) that lack of complete judgment consistency or consensus represents prima facie evidence that at least some judgments are not accurate.

Chow, Shields, and Whittenburg (1989) presented subjects with 56 context-free scenarios that included 12 authoritative sources and 44 pairs of these sources that were likely to be encountered in practice, including combinations of conflicting pairs of authority. Each subject was asked to rate the degree to which a particular pair of sources provided authoritative support. They reported a mean correlation of 0.79 for judgment consistency and a mean correlation of 0.45 for judgment consensus.

Bain and Kilpatrick (1990), also using context-free combinations of authority, asked their subjects to rate the degree to which authoritative support was provided. Two differences between this study and Chow et al. (1989) should be noted. First, as observed by Bain and Kilpatrick(1990), the consensus level reported by Chow et al. (1989) may be overstated because substantial-authority judgments only would be made when there are conflicting authorities and because the presence of pairs of nonconflicting sources would be expected to increase the level of consensus. Therefore, only conflicting combinations of sources were used in Bain and Kilpatrick (1990). Second, Bain and Kilpatrick used several types of authoritative evidence, including single versus single sources, single versus multiple sources, and multiple versus multiple sources. The last two types of authoritative evidence were not examined by Chow et al. (1989). Despite these differences, the reported results of a mean correlation of 0.68 for judgment consistency and a mean correlation of 0.54 for judgment consensus were similar to those of Chow et al. (1989).

A potential limitation of Chow et al. (1989) and Bain and Kilpatrick (1990) is that context-free scenarios were used in both studies. Consequently, the subject was placed in an unnatural environment in which contextual factors, such as the nature of the tax issue, could not inform the required JDM.

Chang and McCarty (1988) also examined the substantial-authority decision, but they presented their subjects with context-specific scenarios in which different combinations of five client data facts were incorporated. Chang and McCarty (1988) reported a mean correlation of 0.75 for judgment consensus, a mean correlation of 0.88 for judgment consistency, and a mean correlation of 0.83 for self-insight into cue usage, thereby making salient the importance of context specificity to tax JDM performance.

APPENDIX B: PROBABILISTIC-JUDGMENT STUDIES

Probabilistic-judgment methods were used in only one study to examine tax professionals' JDM. Cloyd (1993) investigated how tax professionals' probability assessments and client advice are affected by two factors: (1) clients' risk attitudes; and (2) the degree of consistency between clients' financial and tax accounting. Subjects were asked to estimate probabilities for a future IRS audit and for the likelihood of success should the tax position be judicially challenged. Subjects also indicated which tax position they would recommend (favorable or unfavorable to the client) and the extent to which they would encourage the client to adopt a consistent financial accounting treatment. Subjects made their decisions after evaluating information (fourth phase of the tax JDM process) about financial accounting conformity and client risk attitude, both of which were manipulated between subjects. Cloyd (1993) reports that when tax and financial accounting are consistent, the subjects were more likely to estimate a lower probability of a future IRS audit, estimate a higher probability of future successful court defense of the favorable position, and to recommend a tax position that is favorable to the client. Finally, the aggressiveness of the subjects' advice was consistent with the client's risk preference.

APPENDIX C: HEURISTICS-AND-BIAS STUDIES

Ten studies have examined three types of heuristic and biases in tax JDM. Eight of the studies were focussed on the information evaluation phase while the revise-and-rank alternatives phase was the focus of two studies. Of the ten studies, one dealt with hindsight/outcome effects, four with framing, four with belief revision, and one with confirmation proneness. Generally, the results of these heuristic-and-biases studies support the notion that tax professionals use simplified cognitive strategies to cope with the demands of complex tasks suggesting, in turn, that their JDM may be biased in ways that non-tax professionals' judgments and decisions also are biased. However, there also are some apparent differences between tax professionals and others in their use of heuristics.

Hindsight/Outcome Effects

A robust finding in a variety of JDM task contexts is that individuals' judgments about the *prior* likelihood of an event are influenced by knowledge that the event has occurred (See Brown and Solomon 1993). It also has been reported that outcome information often influences appraisals of other persons' performance. The former phenomenon has been called a *hindsight effect/bias* whereas the latter has been called an *outcome effect/bias*. Outcome information clearly has the potential to impact tax JDM. For example, if a tax professional were asked in the presence of outcome information to estimate the probability that a tax court would make a particular ruling, his or her probability likely would be higher if he or she knew the court made that ruling than if he or she did not know the court's decision. Importantly, non-tax JDM research on the hindsight bias suggests that the higher probability would be assessed despite explicit instructions to ignore the outcome information.

Helleloid (1988) examined the impact of outcome information in tax settings. In particular, he developed three tax cases (which were manipulated within subject) involving areas of the tax law which generally require judgments about prior expectations of the taxpayer (e.g., assessment of the accumulated earnings tax). Further, Helleloid (1988) manipulated the outcome information (favorable or unfavorable) on a between-subjects basis. Contrary to his hypothesis, he reported that when the subjects knew the client's outcome but were asked to estimate their client's outcome expectation before the client knew the outcome, the subjects' estimates were not influenced by outcome information. Consistent with his hypothesis, however, when these subjects were asked to recommend a tax treatment based on the outcome information, their recommendations were influenced by the outcomes (i.e., those subjects given favorable outcomes recommended more aggressive positions). Helleloid interpreted this ensemble of results as evidence that tax professionals can use outcome information in a normatively appropriate manner with regard to the evaluation of tax law.

Framing Effects

Whether and the extent to which tax professionals' decisions are affected by the *way* in which an uncertain tax setting is perceived was the focus of four tax JDM studies. The authors of these studies relied on prospect theory (Kahneman and Tversky 1979) to motivate their hypotheses and structure their research design. According to prospect theory, the decision frame (i.e., how the decision is perceived, the possible outcomes of the decision, and the probability associated with each possible outcome) may influence choice. Prospect theory has been invoked to predict, and prior research in a variety of generic and applied settings has shown, that decision makers exhibit risk aversion when decisions are framed as gains but exhibit risk-seeking behavior when decisions are framed as losses. This phenomenon has been called a *reflection effect*. In addition, non-tax JDM research has confirmed that reducing the probability of a prospect (i.e., a gamble) by a constant factor has a greater impact on a decision when an outcome initially was certain, than when it was initially uncertain. This phenomenon has been called a *certainty effect*.

Duncan, LaRue, and Reckers (1989) tested for a reflection effect, as well as other effects, on the aggressiveness of a subject's advice to a client. Specifically, their subjects were asked to make a recommendation about the deductibility of an expense. The withholding position of the client (overpaid or underpaid) was manipulated between subjects, hence the potential expense deduction was framed either as a gain or a loss. These authors also manipulated, between subjects, the probability of a future IRS audit, client risk preference (cautious or aggressive). They measured the subjects' years of experience, technical knowledge, and recent IRS-outcome experience. Weak evidence of a reflection effect was reported as evidenced by the more aggressive advice in the under- vs. the over- withheld position. That is, the subjects' advice was more consistent with risk-seeking behavior when the decision was framed as a loss. Duncan et al. (1989), consistent with other predictions, also reported that more aggressive advice was associated with recent IRS-outcome experience and greater technical tax knowledge. Contrary to their predictions, however, these authors reported that the recommendations were *not* associated either with the probability of an audit or with the subjects' length of experience. Finally, again contrary to predictions, it was reported that the subjects' recommendations were more aggressive when the client's risk preference was cautious vs. aggressive.

Sanders and Wyndelts (1989) used between-subject designs to test for both reflection and certainty effects on subjects' choice of which of two tax treatments to recommend to a client that differed in their aggressiveness. The reflection effect was tested by manipulating both the withholding position (refund or additional payment) of the client and whether the tax issue involved an expense or income. Those cases with a refund (additional payment) withholding position or an expense (income) item were considered to have been framed as a gain (loss) situation. The reported results indicated no significant differences in choices for the withholding-framing manipulation but about one-half of the reported results for the income-expense framing manipulation were consistent with the reflection effect.

Sanders and Wyndelts (1989) tested for a certainty effect by using a between-subjects manipulation of the probabilities associated with the outcomes from two alternative tax treatments. Each tax treatment had two possible outcomes. For one tax treatment, one outcome was certain and positive while the other outcome was uncertain and negative and, for the other tax treatment, both outcomes were uncertain with one being negative and the other being positive. The probabilities of the two alternatives with the positive outcomes were manipulated by giving one subject group two probabilities that were one-half the probabilities for those same two alternatives that were given to the other subject group (e.g., one subject group had an alternative with a certain positive outcome and for the other subject group that probability was 0.50). A certainty effect would be exhibited if the subjects' choices of alternatives were affected by the manipulation of these probabilities by a constant, but affected more by the changes in the probabilities of the certain relative to the uncertain outcomes. The subjects' choices of tax treatment were affected as predicted in four of the five cases by the changes in the probabilities.

Newberry, Reckers, and Wyndelts (1993) also were interested in the reflection effect but, unlike predecessor authors, they manipulated the subjects' frame (gains vs. losses) rather than the clients' frame. Specifically, subjects were required to assess the likelihood that they would prepare and sign a tax return with an ambiguous tax deduction in one of two client conditions (framings). In both conditions, the subjects were told that the client wanted to take the deduction and would consider seeking advice from another tax professional if the subject were not to agree that the deduction should be taken. In one condition, the taxpayer was an existing client while in the other the taxpayer was a potential new client. The existing client (new client) condition was intended to represent a contingent loss (gain) situation to the subject. They also manipulated, between subjects, the prospects of preparer penalty enforcement. Consistent with their hypothesis, the reported results revealed that the subjects in the gain condition were more likely to support an ambiguous deduction than those in the loss condition, which is consistent with the prospect theory prediction of risk aversion behavior for gains and risk seeking behavior for losses. Also consistent with their hypothesis, subjects in the high (low) penalty condition were less (more) likely to support an ambiguous deduction.

Schisler (1994) also tested for a reflection effect using two tax JDM contexts (casualty loss and education expenses; a within-subject manipulation). His between-subject framing manipulation was whether a subject's client was to receive a refund or to pay tax. He also manipulated, between subjects, the risk of an IRS penalty and the client risk preference. Contrary to his hypothesis, there was no significant effect due to IRS penalty. With regard to the reflection effect, the reported results depend on whether the subjects knew the client's risk preference. When the subjects did not know the client's risk preference, no reflection effect was reported, however, when it was known, a reflection effect was observed. This conditional result, however, was not anticipated nor adequately explained.

Belief Revision

Three of the four studies in this section are based on the Hogarth and Einhorn (1992) model of belief adjustment, while the focus of the other study is the Einhorn and Hogarth (1985) model of sequential belief revision. Hogarth and Einhorn (1992) assume that beliefs are revised in sequential judgments tasks by an anchoring-and-adjustment heuristic process. In particular, an initial judgment serves as an anchor which is revised subsequently upon receipt of evidence by adjusting from the anchor. Importantly, the magnitude and direction of the adjustment will be affected by the individual's attitude towards ambiguity. Further, researchers using the model have predicted that revised judgments are subject to an order effect arising from the differential weighting of confirmatory versus non-confirmatory evidence. For example, it has been predicted that under conditions of mixed evidence, confirmatory information will be weighted more heavily when it follows receipt of non-confirmatory information than when it is considered before non-confirmatory information. Such differential weighting produces a recency effect (i.e., the most recent evidence received is given greater weight).

The belief adjustment model's presentation order effects have been examined in three tax JDM studies. Pei, Reckers, and Wyndelts (1990) developed an experimental task in which subjects were asked to analyze a real estate tax reporting issue related to dealer-investor classification. Client information relevant to the decision was presented to the subjects in four units. Each information unit was intended to represent either strong or weak support for, or strong or weak opposition to, the client's preference. One-half of the subjects received the supporting evidence followed by the opposing evidence, whereas the remaining subjects received the same evidence but in the reverse order. They also manipulated, between subjects, the client's preference for either dealer or investor classification. As hypothesized, Pei et al. (1990) reported that the subjects' judgments were affected by the order in which the information was presented. In particular, the recommendations to the client were reported to be more (less) favorable when the positive (negative) evidence was presented last. Contrary to their prediction, however, neither a main effect for client preference nor an interaction effect between client preference and order was found.

In a subsequent study, Pei, Reckers, and Wyndelts (1992), using the same experimental task as in their 1990 study, tested an hypothesized three-way interaction among order, client preference, and experience. As hypothesized, it was found that the more experienced subjects' judgments were affected by presentation order, but not by client preference. In contrast, and also as pre-dicted, less experienced subjects' judgments were found to be affected by client preference but not by presentation order.

Mayper, Kilpatrick, and Anderson (1993) also investigated order effects in a tax JDM review context. These authors examined whether and to what extent the judgments and decisions of subjects acting as *reviewers* are affected by the order in which arguments are presented in tax workpapers. It was hypothe-sized that both the order of information presentation in the workpapers and the workpaper preparer's conclusion documented in the workpapers would affect the subjects' likelihood judgments of whether the deduction in question would be upheld in court and final recommendations regarding the decision. Contrary to predictions, however, no order effects were detected and the work-paper preparer's conclusions affected only the subjects' likelihood judgments, but not their final recommendations.

Helleloid (1989) tested another Einhorn and Hogarth (1985) model of sequential belief revision. In each of two experiments, Helleloid asked his sub-jects to estimate the amount of mileage deduction which they would recom-mend that their client report. Ambiguity was manipulated between subjects by varying the frequency with which the client documented the travel (by day, month or year), with ambiguity assumed to increase as documentation was less frequently made. A critical difference between the two experiments was the amount of information provided to subjects about the client. In the first experiment, in which less client background information was presented, the reported results did not support an ambiguity effect. In contrast, in the second experiment, in which more information was provided, the reported results were consistent with the hypothesized ambiguity effect.

Confirmation Proneness

According to Ross (1977), there is a tendency for individuals to assess the rele-vance, reliability and validity of information based on whether or not it con-firms their initial beliefs. More recently, Klayman and Ha (1987, 1989) have suggested that individuals are prone to employing positive as opposed to neg-ative testing strategies when conducting formal or informal hypothesis tests and that such proneness can be problematic. Johnson (1993) sought to examine the extent to which tax professionals' judgments are consistent with a form of confirmation proneness. Subjects in Johnson's (1993) study were presented with one of two cases in which they had to decide whether a certain amount of compensation paid to a corporate officer was reasonable, and therefore, deductible. The subjects were provided with client facts and authoritative evi-dence and then were asked to state an initial judgement of the probability that the compensation would be judicially supported. Next, the subjects reviewed four court cases and then revised their initial probabilities. The subjects also rated the relevance of each of the four cases to the client's issue and recom-mended a position to the client. The outcomes of the four cases were manipu-lated between subjects by reporting to one-half of the subjects that two of the cases were found in favor of the taxpayer while reporting that the other two cases were found against the taxpayer. The remaining subjects were told opposite outcomes with regard to the same four cases and the order of the favorable/unfavorable cases was manipulated.

Johnson (1993) reasoned that if confirmatory processes were being employed, subjects' relevance ratings would vary with the reported judicial outcome. Her findings were that the subjects rated those cases with reported favorable judicial rulings to the client as *more relevant* than those cases with unfavorable judicial rulings. Also, subjects' relevance ratings were reported to be related to the initial and revised beliefs. Finally, Johnson (1993) reported that those subjects who received a case in a planning (open-fact) setting made judgments which exhibited greater consistency with confirmatory processing than did those subjects who received a case in a compliance (closed-fact) setting.

APPENDIX D: COGNITION AND KNOWLEDGE STUDIES

This set of 13 studies represents 48% of all of the tax JDM studies which meet our conclusion criteria. The three primary areas of interest are: The relationship between knowledge and performance; the relationships among knowledge, incentives and performance; and reasoning processes. The studies include examinations of four of the six tax problem-solving phases, with 10 of the 13 studies investigating the information search and information evaluation phases.

Knowledge and Performance

Kaplan et al. (1988) investigated how professional tax experience interacts with the *ambiguity* of a tax issue to affect tax professionals' judgments. Unambiguous issues were defined as those for which there was a "concrete" law which could be applied to verifiable facts, while ambiguous issues were defined as those for which a concrete law did not exist. Specifically, based on assumed linkages between experience and knowledge, they hypothesized that when facing unambiguous issues, tax professionals' recommendations would not be related to years of or specific experiences (e.g., with the IRS). When facing ambiguous issues, however, it was hypothesized that experience would interact with the probability of an IRS audit and the amount of the deduction conditions such that less experienced tax professionals' judgments would be more affected than more experienced tax professionals' judgments by these two variables.

Kaplan et al.'s (1988) subjects were asked to make a recommendation about the deductibility of depreciation and interest expense with regard to a tax shelter scenario. Ambiguity was manipulated, within subject, such that the deductibility of depreciation expense was ambiguous while the deductibility of interest expense deduction was unambiguous. The probability of an IRS audit (high and low) and the amount of the deductions (high and low) were manipulated within subject. The reported results were consistent with the hypotheses. In addition, these authors reported that subjects with recent favorable IRS encounters made more aggressive recommendations than did those subjects without recent favorable IRS experience.

Bonner, Davis, and Jackson (1992) argued that the relationship between knowledge and performance depends both on the type of knowledge and the type of performance. Based on a review of prior research on knowledge structures, they argued that declarative and procedural technical tax knowledge, declarative and procedural functional business knowledge, and general problem-solving ability would have differing relations to three performance measures (quantity, quality, and a combined quantity-quality) in a corporate tax issue identification task.

As hypothesized, Bonner et al. (1992) reported a positive relation between technical tax knowledge and the quantity and the combined quantity-quality measures of performance, and a positive relationship between the quality measure of performance and the interaction of technical tax knowledge, functional business knowledge, and general problem-solving ability. Their results provide partial support for the hypothesized positive relation between functional business knowledge and the combined quantity-quality measure of performance. Contrary to their hypotheses however, the results did not support a relation between functional business knowledge and the quantity measure of performance or between general problem-solving ability and performance. With regard to the distinction between declarative and procedural knowledge, the results indicated that procedural knowledge was not significantly related to the quantity measure of performance, but both knowledge types were significantly related to the quality and combined quantity-quality measure of performance. They also performed an exploratory analysis of the relationship between learning environment variables and knowledge. These findings primarily were intuitive as formal instruction was found to be related to declarative knowledge while procedural knowledge was related to practical experience.

Bonner, Davis, and Jackson (1994) extended Bonner et al. (1992). Based on psychology research examining the role of memory structures in expertise, they hypothesized that knowledge organization would be related to the quantity of performance, but not to the quality or combined quantity-quality measure. They also investigated whether experts, relative to novices, would have knowledge structures containing more and larger categories into which stimuli are organized and whether the contents of the categories would be based on deeper relationships among the stimuli. They used the same experimental task context and performance measures as in their prior study. Knowledge was measured using response latency data and other approaches employed in psychology. "Experts" and "novices" were identified by splitting subjects into groups based on their continuous performance scores. Analysis was performed using both the mean and median as the basis for splitting.

Bonner et al.'s (1994) reported results were consistent with their hypotheses. Their exploratory analysis uncovered no significant difference between the expert and novice subjects in the number and sizes of stimuli categories. However, consistent with prior non-tax research, they reported that the expert subjects categorized information based on deep structural features (i.e., tax law) while the novices categorizations were based on surface features (e.g., balance-sheet accounts).

Knowledge, Motivation, and Performance

In four studies, investigation of the knowledge-performance relation was expanded to include motivational factors (e.g., incentives) during external information search. Spilker (1995) argued that time pressure motivates tax professionals to focus their information search on the information most likely to be relevant, and that declarative and procedural knowledge have independent effects on information search performance. Subjects performed a computerized information search task in which they identified key words in a topical index which they would use to search for authoritative support for a partnership tax issue. Time pressure was manipulated between subjects (low or high). Subjects were placed into one of three knowledge groups: no/low declarative and procedural knowledge (incoming masters of tax students), high declarative knowledge and no/low procedural knowledge (graduating masters of tax students), and high declarative and procedural knowledge (experienced tax professionals). Declarative knowledge and experience tests were administered as manipulation checks. Performance was assessed based on the number of relevant (as determined by an expert panel) key words selected.

Consistent with Spilker's (1995) interaction hypothesis, time pressure was reported to have had a positive impact on performance for those subjects with high procedural and declarative knowledge, a non-significant positive effect on those subjects with high declarative but no/low procedural knowledge, and a marginally significant negative effect on the performance of the subjects with no/low declarative and procedural knowledge.

Spilker and Prawitt (1995) extend Spilker (1995) by investigating how time pressure and experience interact to affect information search behavior. They assumed that more experienced tax professionals have more sophisticated knowledge structures (e.g., better organized and more completely cross-referenced) which allows them to better filter problem facts and select for processing only those facts which are most likely to contribute to successful information search. Based on this assumption, they made three predictions about how experienced vs. inexperienced tax professionals' information search behavior changes with increased time pressure: (1) decreasing the time spent assimilating the facts of a client situation before utilizing key word indices; (2) decreasing the time spent returning from key word indices to the original client facts; and (3) increasing selectivity in information search.

Rather than measure the actual knowledge structure of their tax professional subjects, they used experience as a proxy for knowledge structure. The experienced and inexperienced subjects in this study were the experienced tax professionals and graduating masters of tax students, respectively, used in Spilker (1995). Each subject conducted information search in two cases, a partnership-related case and a control (international tax) case. A knowledge test indicated that both subject groups had similar levels (quantity) of knowledge of partnership and international tax laws and terminology. Only the experienced subjects, however, had experience in partnership tax, while neither subject group had significant experience in international taxation. Time pressure was manipulated between subjects (low or high). Information search behavior was measured three ways: the number of seconds considering the problem statement before initially entering the index, the amount of time referring to the case facts after initially entering the index, and the average importance of the headings searched per unit of time searching (importance was determined by an expert panel).

The results for the partnership case are consistent with the three predictions. In contrast, two of the three predictions were not supported by the results for the control (international tax) case. A key difference between the two cases is that, while the experienced group had significant partnership tax experience, neither subject group had significant experience in international taxation (but the experienced group had slightly more familiarity with international tax law and terminology). The lack of differential international tax experience could explain why, for the international tax case, no time pressure by experience interactions were detected for two of the three predictions.

Cloyd (1995b) used a knowledge-incentive-effort-performance model to develop hypotheses about their effects on information search performance. Cloyd's subjects performed information search using an on-line authoritative data base similar to those available to tax professionals through CD-ROM. The final product of the experimental task was a computerized notebook which included all of the information gathered and believed by the subjects to represent authoritative support for a particular tax situation. Cloyd gathered numerous performance measures, some of which relate to outcome effectiveness and efficiency (1995a) while others relate to the information search process (1995b). Incentives were manipulated using two levels of accountability. Subjects in the high-accountability condition were told that their notebooks would be reviewed by the instructors at the staff school they were attending during the administration of the experiment while those in the low-accountability condition were told that their notebooks would remain anonymous. Declarative knowledge was measured using a general knowledge test.

Consistent with his hypothesis, Cloyd (1995a) reported a positive effect of accountability on effort duration which was measured as time spent on the task. Inconsistent with his hypotheses, however, there were no significant effects on effort due to prior knowledge or a knowledge-by-accountability interaction. Both accountability, through its positive effect on effort duration, and prior knowledge had significant positive main effects on search effectiveness. In addition, consistent with his predictions, there was a positive interaction effect of prior knowledge and accountability on search effectiveness. That is, the positive effect of prior knowledge and accountability on search effectiveness was significantly greater in the high-accountability group than in the low-accountability group. Finally, prior knowledge had a significant, positive effect on the search efficiency of subjects in the high-accountability condition.

In the second study, Cloyd (1995b) focussed on the information search behaviors of the subjects in the high-accountability condition of Cloyd (1995a). The relationship between declarative knowledge and twenty measures of search behavior were examined. Cloyd (1995b) assessed three types of search behaviors: search strategy, amount and type of information, and information discrimination. Declarative knowledge was reported to be significantly correlated with seventeen of the search behavior measures.

Reasoning Processes

Researchers have reported six studies in which they investigated cognitive reasoning processes, four of which examined analogical reasoning by tax professionals in information search and information evaluation, while tax professionals' similarity judgments in the evaluation of information were the focus of two studies.

In three studies, it was proposed that tax professionals use analogical reasoning when evaluating tax authoritative support. An analogy exists when the relationships among stimuli within a domain are consistent with the relationships among stimuli in a different domain, even though the nature of the stimuli in the two domains differs (Gentner 1982). Analogical reasoning occurs when an individual transfers a solution strategy from a problem in one domain to a target problem in a different domain (Mayer 1992). Such reasoning is likely to be employed in situations which are either new to the individual or when there is no unambiguous solution. When analogical reasoning occurs, knowledge is transferred from the source domain to the target domain. Marchant et al. (1989) proposed a cognitive model of tax problem-solving and suggested that analogy plays an important role both in such tax problem-solving and in the development of tax expertise.

To determine whether tax professionals' behavior is consistent with the model they proposed in Marchant et al. (1989), Marchant et al. (1991, 1992, 1993) designed experimental tasks which would permit them to measure knowledge transferred between one or more authoritative sources and a client problem (target). Specifically, subjects were presented with a set of hypothetical tax statutes and a source which represented a judicial interpretation and application of the statutes to a specific situation. Importantly, the source generally differed in surface similarity from the tax issue facing the client (i.e., the target), but the target and source had structural similarities. The target tax issue then was presented to the subjects and they were asked to identify the key facts, the key tax issues, and to predict how a court would rule on these issues. The subjects could use the source to aid in solving the target problem and such use would be consistent with analogical reasoning. Knowledge transfer was deemed to exist if the key facts, key issues, or the predicted court case outcome for the target were the same as the source.

The reported results in Marchant et al. (1991, 1992, 1993) have, for the most part, been inconsistent with the predictions. Based on psychology findings, each study predicted that experts would utilize analogical reasoning to a greater extent and more appropriately than would novices. The experts in these studies were tax professionals with tax experience, while the novices were tax students with no professional tax experience.

Marchant et al. (1991) predicted that experts would use analogical reasoning to a greater extent than novices and, as predicted, experts appeared to transfer more from a structurally similar source analog than did the novices. Contrary to their prediction, however, when the source was presented in a problem-solving context (i.e., subjects were asked to predict the solution to the source before given the correct outcome) or when multiple appropriate sources were provided, the novices exhibited greater transfer than did the experts.

Marchant et al. (1992) predicted that: (1) Knowledge transfer would be greater with complete sources than with no sources for both experts and novices; (2) Knowledge transfer would be greater with no source than with an incomplete source for both experts and novices (where an incomplete source is similar on the surface to, but structurally different from, the target problem); (3) Given a complete source, experts would transfer more knowledge than would novices; and (4) With an incomplete source, experts would not transfer as much knowledge as would the novices. Weak support was reported for the first two predictions, but no support was reported for the latter two predictions. They suggested that one possible explanation for their results may be that the experienced professionals were exhibiting the effect of client advocacy (i.e., a state of mind in which a tax professional feels his or her primary loyalty belongs to the taxpayer). Such advocacy may have led the subjects to discount the importance of the ruling in the sources since, in the study, the sources always contained unfavorable results for the taxpayer.

Marchant et al. (1993) extended Marchant et al. (1992) by conducting two experiments. In the first experiment, they predicted that the extent of transfer from a source to a target would be an interactive function of the tax professional's expertise and the similarity between the source and target, in which experts (novices) would transfer more of the source to the target when the source and target had structural (surface) similarity. The reported results were not consistent with the interaction prediction. Both expert and novice subjects exhibited a high (low) degree of transfer from the source to the target when the source and target had structural (surface) similarity. The second experiment in Marchant et al. (1993) was intended to test whether the unexpected results of the first experiment were due to a client advocacy effect in which the extent to which tax professionals would transfer information from the source to the target would depend on whether they predicted that the court's ruling on the source would be favorable or unfavorable to the client. Specifically, Marchant et al. (1993) argued that expert tax professionals' degree of transfer would be more affected than would novice tax professionals' transfer by their prediction of the court's ruling on the source case. Thus, they predicted a three-way interaction among tax professional expertise, source-target similarity, and the tax professional's prediction of the source case (favorable or unfavorable). Several sets of tests were reported which, in total, indicated that their predictions were supported, although the expertise effect appeared to be stronger for the transfer of surface similarity than for structural similarity.

Krawczyk, Marchant, and Robinson (1994) extended the investigation of analogical reasoning to the information search phase of tax JDM. Psychology research has identified three constraints on analogical reasoning: (1) Fact similarity limits consideration to those sources whose facts closely correspond to the facts in the target problem; (2) Issue consistency restricts consideration to those sources for which the underlying issue corresponds to the target problem; and (3) Desired outcome limits consideration of potential sources according to whether the outcome is desired by the decision maker. These authors predicted that fact similarity would be the dominant constraint during the selection phase (information search). Three experiments were used to manipulate various levels of issue and fact consistency and outcomes (favorable vs. unfavorable). The experimental task required subjects to rank the applicability of a set of one or more authoritative rules with respect to a target problem. In all of the experiments, the results were consistent with the prediction that fact similarity would be the most important factor in the applicability determinations of the subjects, although this was somewhat mediated by the direction of the outcome.

A related reasoning process used in the tax JDM cognition studies is that proposed by Tversky's (1977) model of *similarity judgments*. Tversky proposed that the judged similarity of two objects is based on a comparison of the common and distinct features of the two objects. Specifically, judged similarity is a positive function of the number of common features and a negative function of the number of dissimilar features. This model further suggests that certain biases may occur during the similarity judgment process (e.g., similarity judgments will *not* be symmetric when the amount of unique information known about two objects is not equal). This model proposes that individuals will use one object as the source and the other as the target, and the features of the source will control the comparison. If the source were to have more unique features than the target, the pair would be judged less similar than if the target were to have been used as the source (i.e., if the comparison had been made in the opposite direction). Tversky (1977) also predicted that the impact of each common and unique feature is determined by its salience, with salience being determined by diagnosticity. The diagnosticity of any feature is influenced by the objects under consideration. The higher the degree to which a feature can discriminate one object from the other objects, the higher is that feature's diagnosticity. Two studies investigated the similarity judgments of tax professionals in the evaluation of tax authority using Tversky's (1977) model.

Schadewald and Robinson (1993) investigated the similarity judgments of tax professionals using Tversky's (1977) similarity model. Schadewald and Robinson (1993) developed a task based on I.R.C. §482 which requires taxpayers to account for intercompany sales using a price that is based on a comparable sale between independent companies. Application of this tax law would require similarity judgments to be formulated with regard to various sales. The experimental task required that subjects evaluate the features of other products sold and make judgments regarding the similarity of those sales to the client's sale. The diagnosticity of the product features was manipulated within subjects. Contrary to their predictions, the authors reported that the subjects' similarity judgments were not affected by the diagnosticity of the features. In addition, they reported that the subjects' self-reported decision rules suggested that they may be using a simpler judgment strategy than the feature-matching model of Tversky (1977).

Davis and Mason (1994) also investigated the similarity judgements of tax professionals using Tversky's (1977) similarity model. Their study is distinguished from Schadewald and Robinson (1993) since they examined several aspects of the similarity model and authoritative information rather than client-fact patterns were evaluated. Davis and Mason (1994) developed two experimental tasks, each using a different case context. In one case, the client required a determination of whether a class of workers was employees or independent contractors. In the second case, the client required a determination of the treatment of a financial instrument as either debt or equity. In each experiment, the authors manipulated, between subjects, the amount of unique information between the court case and the client's facts (low and high), and the outcome of the court case (favorable and unfavorable). Client advocacy and the direction of the subjects' comparison (court case to client or client to court case) were measured independent variables. Also, subjects' experience and knowledge, and in the first experiment whether they were employed as a tax practitioner or IRS revenue agent, were measured and used as covariates. Three dependent variables were used: Subjects' judgments about the similarity of the court case and the client's facts, subjects' ratings of the importance of the common and distinctive features of the court case and client's facts to their similarity judgments, and subjects' rating of the likelihood of success of the taxpayer-favored tax treatment if it were to be judicially challenged.

Consistent with their hypotheses, the interaction of client advocacy and the court case outcome was significantly and positively related to the weights assigned to common features. In addition, common feature weights were significantly and positively associated with the similarity judgments. Contrary to their hypotheses, however, the interaction of client advocacy and the court case outcome was not related to either the unique or the combined feature weights (i.e., the difference between the unique and the common weightings) and these feature weights did not significantly impact similarity judgments. As hypothesized, the weights of the unique features in experiment one depended upon the direction of comparison such that when the source of the comparison had more unique information than did the target, the unique feature weights were higher than when the source of the comparison had less unique information than did the target. In experiment two, however, no support was found for this source-target asymmetry effect. Since the results of the two experiments are inconsistent, it is unclear whether the antecedent conditions for asymmetric judgments in tax practice exist. Finally, consistent with their hypothesis, Davis and Mason (1994) reported that the likelihood of success judgments were an interactive function of the court case outcome and the similarity judgments about the court case and the client's problem.

6

REALLY USEFUL
RESEARCH

CHRISTINE PURDIE AND MICHAEL L. ROBERTS

"Good morning, Pooh," said Owl.
"Many happy returns of Eeyore's birthday," said Pooh.
"Oh, is that what it is?"
"What are you giving him, Owl?"
"What are you giving him, Pooh?"
"I'm giving him a Useful Pot to Keep Things In, and I wanted to ask you — — —"
"Is this it?" said Owl, taking it out of Pooh's paw.
"Yes, and I wanted to ask you — — —"
"Somebody has been keeping honey in it," said Owl.
"You can keep anything in it," said Pooh earnestly. "It's Very Useful like that."

—A. A. Milne

Professional tax accountants, and the firms they belong to, are currently in the midst of a sea change. In the past, command of the intricacies of the tax laws guaranteed that the tax accountant would be consulted by clients on complex matters of tax compliance and on the tax angles of prospective transactions. Today, however, clients are no longer content with a tax accountant who is merely a technical tax expert. Clients are looking for something more: a Business/Tax Consultant.

This new and improved Business/Tax Consultant should have a commanding knowledge of the tax law, to be sure, but that is just the beginning. The ideal Business/Tax Consultant should also have a commanding knowledge of business management principles, financial strategies, global business practices, and industry-specific practices and opportunities. The ideal Business/Tax Consultant should be as effective when addressing the board of directors as when interpreting IRS regulations. The ideal Business/Tax Consultant should be resourceful enough to periodically develop and present new strategies for trimming an additional percent or two off the client's effective tax rate, and when called on to save a pending acquisition, the ideal Business/Tax Consultant should be creative enough to sketch out a plan for a quadruple-reverse-nontaxable merger—with a twist... and should always answer the client's phone call on the first ring.

Despite these somewhat exaggerated expectations, the message inherent in the description of an ideal Business/Tax Consultant, the message that has been clearly sent by the business community and clearly received by tax accountants in public practice, is a demand for more "value-added" client service. As a consequence, firms are placing increasing emphasis on tax consulting and planning engagements rather than more routine compliance engagements.

In addition, practitioners are being encouraged to be more "proactive" in anticipating client needs, rather than waiting for the client to request assistance. Clients are asking their tax accountants to continuously monitor and provide advice for their business and to apply cutting-edge industry-specific knowledge and advice. Also, clients want that advice communicated in a style that is clear and concise.

As professional tax accountants develop their strategies for meeting these escalating client expectations, the current situation presents a timely opportunity for synergy between Practice and the Academy. By applying scientific research methods to the practical problems of professional tax accountants, behavioral tax researchers can provide valid information about how to achieve the new goals that clients are setting for Practice. By collaborating, tax practitioners and behavioral tax researchers have the potential to bring together their interests, knowledge, skills, and abilities to create innovative solutions for today's practice problems. Like Pooh's Very Useful Pot, what is currently needed is Really Useful Research to address the very real challenges affecting Practice and to help produce the new generation of Business/Tax Consultants.

The purposes of this chapter are to identify specific areas in which behavioral research can address tax practice problems and issues and to discuss potentially relevant directions, methodologies, and contributions of research that can produce "really useful" results for practice. We also discuss some of the institutional and environmental constraints that currently exist within both Practice and the Academy and offer some suggestions for overcoming or at least making an end run around those constraints.

THE CHALLENGES OF PROFESSIONAL TAX PRACTICE

Consider the challenges of professional practice from the perspective of a tax partner in a large accounting firm:

Neil Smythe has just been informed of his promotion to managing tax partner in a medium-sized office of a Big Six firm. Having received word of his promotion, he is in a reflective mood. Alone in his office, he leans back in his high-back, black leather executive chair, and thinks back to when he first joined the firm....

"Things were a lot simpler then... there was a lot more certainty about what was expected.... I knew I would spend the first couple of years doing a lot of tax returns. If I worked hard, put in enough hours and was good enough, I'd get promoted right along to senior manager. Then, if I could demonstrate the right people skills and keep my clients happy, I could count on making partner... a pretty fixed career path.

Not that it was easy. Only one in ten ever made it to partner. Most of those who didn't weren't willing to pay the price. Or couldn't. There were a lot of long hours... a lot of late nights and weekends, especially around filing deadlines. And the more hours billed, the better.

Of course, there was a lot of uncertainty, too. There was so much to learn. I don't think I really felt comfortable that I knew enough about anything for the first two or three years. I had to ask a lot of questions.... Sometimes I didn't think I could ever learn as much as the partners and managers. Some of them were unbelievable... mention any topic, code section, or case, and it was like ... a photographic memory. Very intimidating.

If you were lucky, you might get a senior manager or partner to adopt you and make sure you got the right assignments, someone who would keep you on target and stand behind you if you made a major mistake, which was inevitable. Good ol' Ben Kenobi. What would have happened to me if not for him? He sure bailed me out on that consolidated return that time.... If not for Ben, I would never have made it this far, that's for sure.

Eventually though, I learned enough to begin supervising new staff. I began reviewing their work, and after awhile I realized that I knew more than a lot of other people. The managers and partners seemed to like me and let me know they thought I was doing a good job.... Of course, some of them seemed more interested in their own power trips (I'll never forgive Vince McGill for bawling me out in front of half the staff!), but they were that way to everybody....

After a while, I started to get more research and planning opportunities, like working on the front-end of a merger and acquisition deal, doing year-end planning for a Fortune 100 company, and helping out with the personal financial planning for the chief financial officer of one of the firm's big clients. Those two years in the Washington National Office were a tremendous learning experience, too. I learned more about how to work with the tax law in the first six months in National than all the other years put together.

A lot has changed since those days.... For one thing, the firm was almost all male back then. Now over half our new hires are women.... Everything was manual then, too—no computers, except for the big mainframes. High-tech was a ten-key with a digital display. PCs hadn't even been invented. All the returns were done by hand and then typed. Things are a lot easier today with all the new technology, return software and electronic research databases. What would the partners from 20 years ago do today? All that tax knowledge... what they depended on having stored away in their heads... now any junior staffer with a notebook PC can instantly produce every court case ever decided on an issue.

At least when I was coming up, I knew that if I could survive the hours, if I was good enough and worked hard enough, eventually it would be my turn to help run the business, to make decisions about resources and strategic directions. Not that there were many strategic decisions to make.... The business was a lot more stable back then. Being a partner in those days was easy compared to today. Clients were loyal, liability concerns were virtually nonexistent, the economy was good, profits were steady, competition was more professional.... What an old fogy—'life in the good old days'.... Still, it did seem easier then....

These days, there's so much more pressure. Not so much from dealing with the technical part of the law or with the complexity of the transactions—that's always been there—that's really the fun part... but the competition is so much more aggressive... or maybe it was that way all the time, and I just never saw that side of it.... But, no, I think the business really has changed. There's a lot more pressure about profits. It's harder to grow now. And clients want more. I'm not even sure they know what they want... but whatever it is, we've got to figure it out and give it to them or they'll look someplace else. That's clear enough....

Well, thank goodness we've got a talented staff. They're as bright and hard working as ever.... I just hope we can hang on to them—too many of the best ones leave just when they've become real contributors.... We've got to figure out how to give the managers and staff what they need... to involve them more with clients, let them see how those of us who've been around for awhile work through problems... and help them develop so that they can contribute as soon as possible.... The new technology and access to information is great, but the big question is what can our bright young people do with that technology and information. That's still the most important challenge we face.... Having all the databases in the world doesn't help if the consultants can't apply that information to solving clients' problems... or even decide what the problem is in the first place. If only we could take the experience of our best people and bottle it somehow....

Then, we have to help them learn to listen to the clients and to anticipate service opportunities. That's the key. We've got to figure out how to give the clients what they want and need... and to help our people think that way, too. If we can just focus on that, we'll be all right...."

This reflection suggests that tax accountants, accustomed to predictable career patterns based on stable client service patterns, are beginning to respond to increased competitive pressures and to recent shifts in clients' expectations. In the past, career progression for tax accountants in public firms was "up or out" with a fairly fixed path to partner for those with the abilities and commitment. As experience increased, so did responsibilities. As responsibilities increased, learning on the job was essential for the individual's continued survival.

To survive to partner, a tax accountant had to learn and exhibit a portfolio of specific skills and, equally important, demonstrate those skills in a specific sequential progression. At the first level (staff tax accountant), this progression emphasized learning to accept direction and learning to perform in an unstructured environment, i.e., a work environment that allowed trial, error, and correction. The second level (tax senior) emphasized an ability to learn to manage others' work and to learn technical mastery of complex rules and procedures. The third and fourth levels (manager and senior manager) placed increased emphasis on learning to communicate effectively with peers, staff, partners, and clients; learning to manage broader personnel and workflow challenges (e.g., evaluating staff and scheduling client assignments); and learning to create and develop innovative solutions to complex technical problems. The fifth level (partner) emphasized learning to develop new business opportunities and to manage resources. Each level required continued personal growth in time and stress management and in balancing work and personal goals and responsibilities.

Though tax accountants have always had to respond to change in both their daily work and in managing their careers, various forces of change—some governmental, some societal, some economic—have been influencing the practice of tax accounting for the past decade or so and are currently affecting firms as well as individual practitioners. We have selected three facets of these recent changes in tax practice to discuss opportunities for research.

First, the nature of tax accounting practice has changed in recent years and is continuing to evolve. The most striking changes surround responses to clients' expectations for the tax accountant to be a business adviser to the client rather than merely a source of technical tax compliance and information. Placing increased emphasis on the role of business adviser or consultant creates a need for individual tax accountants and firms to re-think the traditional role of the professional tax accountant and to identify ways in which entry-level tax professionals can learn to be expert business/tax advisers. This change has the potential to dramatically affect tax practice and tax accountants' professional development.

Second, there is an emerging need to develop new approaches to managing the business of maintaining and growing a tax practice. Tax accountants are subject to the same business challenges as other service-providers, including hiring, retaining, developing, motivating, and rewarding workers; satisfying customers; billing and collecting for work performed; keeping up-to-date with technological changes; and developing new "products" and/or new markets. Changing client service needs implies changes in the functioning of the tax practice to meet those new needs. This, in turn, implies that the tax professionals who are in charge of managing and allocating the resources of the practice should develop strategies for effectively dealing with these changes and be innovative and flexible in implementing new practice methods to enable the practice to retain market share and grow into new markets. For example, advances in computer hardware and software have allowed some routine aspects of tax compliance to be standardized, streamlined, and even out-sourced by some firms. As technology and communications continue to change, new practice management methods should be developed to use these new tools to improve client service.

Changes in practice management also should meet the needs of the professionals that make up the firm, a challenge that is just as important to the long-run success of the practice as meeting client needs. For example, as the demographics (gender, age, race and ethnicity) and lifestyles of individuals who comprise professional tax staffs change, innovative approaches for personal learning and development, including but not limited to technical learning and development, should be designed to ensure that the intellectual resources and assets of the practice continue to be available to support the practice's client service goals.

Third, professional tax practice requires individuals to develop varying degrees of technical expertise in interpreting and applying the tax law. Technical expertise has long been the hallmark of professional tax accountants. It has been their "bread and butter," their raison' d'être. As the underlying body of tax law continues to change and to grow, both in volume and in complexity, the strategies and methods that tax practitioners develop for coping with technical demands become increasingly important for their development into competent professionals and for their individual satisfaction with both the job and their contributions.

Each of these facets of change, and implications for practice and research, are explored in more depth below. We discuss practice questions in each area—the tax accountant as business adviser, practice manager, and technical expert—with the goal of establishing a context and an agenda for researchable topics and research questions that can address issues of interest to tax practitioners, particularly those charged with managing a tax practice.

BUSINESS ADVISER

Clients often request that the accountant take a more active role in advising the client about their business, in addition to providing solutions to questions about technical accounting and tax issues. Clients want their CPAs, including their tax accountants, to know the ins and outs of their industry and their operations.

For example, suppose a client contacts their tax accountant for assistance with a pending acquisition. The client may have already developed a tentative financing plan for either a taxable or nontaxable merger. Assume the tax accountant responds in one of the following ways: (1) verifies the tax effects of the client's tentative plan, (2) creates a financing plan that would be more advantageous than the one the client has already developed such as analyzing the gains/losses under various combinations of financing plans and determining that (a) a nontaxable merger could result in substantial tax savings over the taxable merger that the client has developed *or* (b) due to the presence of mitigating factors (e.g., net operating loss carryovers, the advantages of stepped-up basis, freedom from restrictions on subsequent transfers, etc.) a taxable merger could result in substantial tax savings over the nontaxable merger that the client has developed, or (3) assists the client in determining that the target company is not the best "fit" for the client due to differences in business philosophies or industry trends. To the extent that the tax accountant provides advice that is either more advanced or insightful in technical tax terms than the client's proposed plan (as in the second response), or provides valuable business advice "outside the box" of the technical tax solutions (as in the third response), then the tax accountant can demonstrate "value added" to the client.

Several barriers may inhibit tax accountants from effectively adopting a business adviser's role. Tax accountants may be reluctant to choose an industry in which to develop their expertise. Selecting one industry in which to specialize contains an inherent opportunity risk that the tax accountant may, at some future point, look back on the decision with regret because the chosen industry did not grow as much as anticipated and therefore the tax accountant's career and importance to the firm was limited.

Also, tax accountants may be (justifiably) proud of their mastery of the complexities of the arcane technicalities of tax law. This pride may lead to an attitude that values the acquisition of technical tax knowledge and skills over more general business and industry specific knowledge and skills. Learning and applying general, industry-specific, and client-specific business knowledge and skills should be regarded as just as important and challenging as acquiring and applying technical tax expertise.

In addition, the volume of knowledge necessary for tax accountants to gain expertise in general business and industry consulting is in addition to an already daunting body of technical tax knowledge needed to advise clients about the tax aspects of their businesses. There are practical limits to both the total quantity of relevant business, industry, and tax knowledge that tax accountants can gain and to the speed with which this body of knowledge can be mastered for application.

Similarly, application of these paradigms—general business consulting, industry consulting, and tax technical consulting—to business situations requires a sometimes subtle and intricate interweaving of different sets of knowledge and skills. Whether business management principles and strategies, industry considerations, or technical tax issues dominate the solution to a specific problem and how tax accountants' knowledge and skills converge, diverge or interact among these three paradigms when tax accountants are engaged in problem solving, research, and planning for clients are intriguing issues for both practice and research.

Other key issues in the business adviser area include:

• What are clients' expectations for business/tax advising? Are clients asking for the impossible, a SuperTaxPerson, or are there legitimate issues of omission in the scope of past or current technical tax engagements and solutions being offered, collectively, by tax accountants? If clients are dissatisfied with the advice and services currently offered, then what, exactly, are the nature of the services that the business community expects—can they be identified or defined in terms that can be acted upon, i.e., researched, modeled, measured, taught and/or implemented?

- Assuming client expectations can be defined, what are the implications for university and continuing education? For example, how do we need to change the learning actions (and materials) in tax courses? In non-tax business courses? Or can we simply add courses to integrate the technical tax and the non-tax body of knowledge in existing courses? Should we focus attention more on formal education efforts or should we target on-the-job learning and concentrate on developing better mentoring and coaching systems for practice? What other (new) approaches might we create?

- On a firm-by-firm basis, what industry-specific knowledge and skills are needed to meet clients' industry-specific needs?

- Should individual tax accountants be encouraged to specialize in a particular industry? If so, at what point in their career?

- Should industry-specific learning be integrated with general business advising and technical tax learning from the very beginning of the tax accountant's career? Or do individuals require a certain period of assimilation and "practice-time" (similar to pilots who are graded according to their "air time") before moving on to the next phase of development?

- What effect do individual differences in learning style have on acquisition and application of these different sets of knowledge and skills (i.e., general business consulting, industry-specific consulting, and technical tax consulting)? Are certain learning strategies for integrating, retaining, and applying the knowledge and skills of these three paradigms more effective for a majority of tax professionals?

PRACTICE MANAGER

Despite the demanding technical requirements, at the end of the day, the business of tax accounting is a people business:
People make contacts and keep in touch with clients.
People research and answer clients' questions.
People are the single biggest asset of the firm
And the single biggest expense of the firm.
People either move up or move on.
People either create innovative solutions for clients
Or they don't.
People are the key to growing… or slowing.

Because *relations among people are voluntary*, being in the people business means that practice managers should continuously monitor and seek to improve relations with people *inside* and *outside* the practice (i.e., the firm). To do this, practice managers should identify the needs of people within the firm as well as the needs of people outside the firm. For example, public accounting firms have traditionally experienced high turnover rates, mostly among staff accountants in their first few years of practice. The relatively high turnover rate raises the question, among others, whether the needs of recently-hired tax accountants are being met and, if not, who is or should be addressing them. In the present practice model, tax accountants in their first few years with a firm are often closely supervised on a day-to-day basis by individuals with only a year or two more seniority. Thus, while the junior tax accountant may receive sufficient guidance to complete daily assignments, the individual's need for mentoring, i.e., modeling skilled professional performance, giving helpful feedback, providing encouragement, imparting career advice, etc., may be lacking. Similarly, some young people may be forced into the role of supervising others who are experiencing difficulties in their personal lives (e.g., divorce, single parenting, illness) that the supervisor has not experienced. To meet the needs of people inside the firm, the tax accountant as practice manager should be prepared for these contingencies. While these kinds of issues may appear trivial, the loss of experienced professionals who have been trained at great expense and who have valuable relations with clients because of insensitivity to such matters increases start-up costs for replacements on the client service team and increases recruiting and training expenditures.

Meeting the needs of people inside the firm also implies that individuals' expectations and assumptions about a variety of factors associated with the workplace environment, including hours and overtime; the scope and quality of performance; available support from senior and junior consultants, personal computer hardware, software, and technical support (e.g., network management); and cooperative attitudes are in sync with the expectations and assumptions of the firm and of the client. For example, a recent hire into a tax department may assume that a close mentoring system is in place and that the work will immediately involve a series of complex and interesting tax planning engagements. If the firm's expectations are that the new hire will spend the first six to 18 months in a pool of first year staff who rotate among senior consultants and managers while gaining experience gradually through (what appears to the new hire to be a haphazard) assignment of tax return preparation, then this mutual mistake in expectations likely will result in losing the individual.

In addition to reducing turnover costs, there is a larger issue of client service that depends on an atmosphere of professional courtesy and respect within the professional firm. Developing an atmosphere in which people are comfortable with, and rewarded for, volunteering ideas and engaging in brainstorming meetings without fear of repercussion or ridicule and rewarded for spending extraordinary amounts of personal time and energy to meet goals and deadlines are as important to the larger issue of practice management as are issues of anticipating and satisfying clients' business and technical needs. Care must be taken to develop formal and informal, as well as economic and noneconomic, incentive systems that reward and encourage positive behaviors. This is critically important not only for short-run client benefits but also for the long-run well-being and success of the people within the firm. The current business trend of "downsizing" so as to "run lean and mean," for example, may work wonders for short-run profitability but may have disastrous long-term effects by burning out talented people within the firm.

Satisfying the needs of clients, people outside the practice, obviously includes providing the technical tax, general business, and industry-specific consulting they expect. In today's environment it also means anticipating those needs rather than merely reacting to them. Clients are looking for tax accountants who will approach them with new ideas for tax savings and business opportunities rather than tax accountants who sit by the telephone waiting to leap into action only when and if the client calls. Clients also are placing increasing importance on the clarity, style, and frequency of communications from their tax accountant regarding technical and business advice. In addition, today's clients expect the professionals they engage to be capable of interacting in more diverse cultural settings than in the past. This, in turn, suggests a need for a more diverse and culturally aware group of professional tax accountants inside the firm. Thus, the expectations and relations between people inside and outside the firm are dynamic forces that practice managers must continually monitor.

In addition to people issues, the economics of practice management are important to maintaining and developing a successful tax practice. Identifying and choosing appropriate business strategies for accepting and retaining clients, developing winning proposals for new clients, determining which industries or products to target for future growth, investing in research and development to create new products and professional learning and performance support systems, choosing and implementing appropriate productivity measures, and determining effective compensation packages all have direct economic consequences for the tax practice's "bottom line" as well as behavioral and motivational consequences for people. Research can help provide the data for practice managers to evaluate the alternatives, to make informed decisions, to make strategic corrections, to evaluate the results, and to formulate new policies and approaches.

Some of the key tax practice management questions are:

- What is "productivity?" How best to measure productivity? How best to increase productivity, both for individuals and for practice units? Are "billable hours" a valid measure for individual contribution? Are they the best measure? What incentives and behaviors follow from various measures? What are the costs/benefits of various incentive options?

- How do we balance the stress of tax practice and being "on call" for clients with the promotion of healthy life-styles for professional tax accountants?

- How do we increase the percentage of higher-value-added consulting engagements relative to lower-value-added compliance engagements? Do "compliance" engagements necessarily involve less value-added services to clients than "consulting" or "planning" engagements? Is there an appropriate or best product mix? If so, and if it involves a change from the current mix, what investments are needed to achieve the preferred mix?

- Should we develop entry-level professionals' consulting abilities with or without a two to three year apprenticeship in compliance activities? And if changes are needed in current approaches, what are the alternatives and what are their respective features and costs?

- What are the costs and benefits of flex-time and part-time arrangements to meet the seasonal work compression problem of most tax practices?

- What changes are needed to retain professionals who are dropping out of professional practice? What are the costs and benefits of making the changes, or of not making them?

- How effective have the increased marketing efforts of professional tax accounting firms been in recent years? What measures might be used? What marketing strategies would be received positively by prospective clients? Do these approaches require the participation of "line" partners, managers, and staff, or should marketing be left to marketing professionals? What indications or evidence exists or can be generated by research?

- What cognitive and affective abilities are associated with effective practice development? Are these abilities found among tax accountants to the same degree as the abilities associated with effective performance in technical tax tasks? Can these skills be learned?

- What are (might be) key measures for effective practice managers and mentors? What techniques or strategies are needed for developing effective practice managers and for developing effective mentors?

TECHNICAL EXPERT

When considering the role of the tax accountant as a technical expert, the first step is a needs assessment or business analysis to identify the tax accountants' clients' needs. Technical expertise is not practiced in a vacuum, and the kind and degree of technical expertise should flow from an assessment of the tax accountant's clientele. This implies that the definition of and implications for providing and developing technical expertise will differ among accounting firms because of the wide differences in clientele, mission, and business strategy. For example, learning to work competently with the numerous IRS forms and filing requirements for individual taxpayers entails specific knowledge and expertise (depending on the complexity involved). Yet, this type of expertise may not be very important in a firm whose clientele is primarily large corporations. The ability to analyze judicial opinions to distinguish how differences in facts and legal reasoning affect judges' opinions may be a required skill for all tax accountants in a firm that specializes in litigation support or other areas in which case law predominates but may be a much less important skill in a firm whose clientele is primarily individual taxpayers with less complex tax problems.

Similarly, the definition of (and implications for providing and developing) technical expertise among individual tax accountants will depend on the individual's role within the firm as well as the individual's interests and choices among possible career paths. A tax accountant who specializes in personal financial planning will need knowledge and skills that differ from those of a tax accountant who specializes in international assignments or mergers and acquisitions or banking. The specific definition of individual expertise in each of these areas likely will involve some overlapping as well as some nonoverlapping knowledge and skills. That is, experts in each of these areas may rely on some common tax rules and planning principles (e.g., the general advisability of accelerating deductions and deferring income recognition, using income splitting to minimize progressive tax rates, including the effects of "implicit" taxes on investments), but expertise in personal financial planning may depend more on the tax accountant's skills in recognizing clients' motives for investments and catering to clients' emotional needs while expertise in banking may depend more on the tax accountant's skill in creating solutions to conflicting regulatory provisions.

Though specific discussions and recommendations for developing technical expertise should be based on the results of needs assessment and business analysis, we can distinguish, generally, three levels of technical expertise for tax accounting. *Novices* include entry-level tax accountants and others (e.g., recent, experienced audit transfers) who have not yet acquired the basic, foundation level of technical tax knowledge and skills required for routine tax engagements and to supervise less-experienced staff. The normal time for promotion to tax "senior," i.e., approximately two to four years of tax practice, is one indicator of the amount of time required to progress through the learning process and gain this foundation level of knowledge and skills, depending on the variety of assignments undertaken during that time.

Intermediate experts are tax practitioners who have acquired the basic, foundation level of technical tax knowledge and skills required for routine tax engagements. Categorizing tax accountants as intermediate experts could be accomplished via a positive classification process, i.e., the identification of the knowledge and skills needed for routine tax engagements and the development and application of valid performance measures. Alternatively, tax accountants could be classified as possessing intermediate expertise by default, i.e., a negative classification of tax accountants who are neither novices nor recognized experts. For example, since the acquisition of expertise across a wide spectrum of human activities (from music to physics) has been estimated to require at least ten years of sustained practice, tax generalists with more than two and less than ten years of experience could be considered intermediate experts by this definition.

In contrast to the first two categories, tax *technical experts* are individuals who consistently achieve outstanding performance in interpreting and applying the tax law to clients' problems. Experts include both individuals who are *specialists* in particular industries, transactions, or compliance areas as well as individuals who are *generalists*, but whose technical performance, whether due to outstanding knowledge or ability or some combination, is consistently outstanding. Usually technical experts will be recognized as such by peers, and perhaps by clients. Experts may also be recognized by their outstanding performance as authors of technical writings or outstanding performance as continuing education instructors.

Of course, the above descriptions beg two questions (at least): what is expertise and how do we know it when we see it? That is, what specifically comprises the basic, foundation level knowledge and skills needed for routine tax engagements that, in turn, constitute intermediate technical expertise (as well as the knowledge and skills that constitute technical expertise)? Second, what is "outstanding performance" for recognizing expertise, i.e., what criteria currently exist or can be developed for distinguishing performance that is above or below the theoretical and practical distinction between "expert" performance and merely "good" performance? Behavioral tax researchers can help practitioners answer both of these questions.

In addition to answering these fundamental questions, researchers can identify the developmental stages of knowledge and skill acquisition. For example, are there stages of knowledge and skill application that can be used to describe the progression of novices to intermediate expertise either across firm and practice types or within categories of firms and practices? Are there clearly identifiable learning stages for acquiring the cognitive concepts and structures that underlie much of the tax laws and rules—concepts such as income, deductible expenses, basis, gain and loss recognition, income shifting? Are these elements of tax knowledge being learned in the abstract or in application to concrete situations?

Additionally, are the individual differences in learning style that have been observed in the general population present among tax accountants? If so, how (if at all) do these differences in learning style affect the progression of tax accountants from novices to intermediate experts and from intermediate experts to experts?

The full panoply of research methodologies can be brought to bear on the issues associated with the acquisition and application of technical expertise by tax accountants. Descriptive, theory-building research can be used to identify experts and to develop theories of how experts' performance differs from that of novices and intermediate experts. Field research is needed to describe and provide empirical evidence of the effects of environmental factors in the acquisition and application of technical expertise. Experimental and quasi-experimental research is needed to test theories of technical knowledge and skill acquisition and performance.

Examples of specific researchable issues and questions include:

· Is there a baseline, core, or foundation body of technical knowledge (i.e., a tax technical taxonomy) needed for competency in professional practice, and by whom (e.g., entry level, beginning supervisory [light tax senior], advanced supervisory [heavy senior or light manager], practice manager/developer [senior manager/partner])? If so, what elements constitute this core or taxonomy?

· Specifically, what knowledge and skills are needed and at what different levels of development?

· What levels of expertise are needed? What levels are optimal?

- What is the relationship between knowledge and application (missing/magic links), e.g.: Can knowledge and application skill be accelerated, and if so, how can this be accomplished? What is the relation between, and implications of, differences in individual learning styles (broadly defined) and knowledge acquisition? What is the relation between differences in individual learning styles and application?

- What is the relationship between knowledge and information management/research: Can skill in information management be accelerated and, if so, how? What is the relation between, and implications of, differences in individual learning styles (broadly defined) and information management? What is the relation between differences in individual learning styles and application of information acquired through information management/research?

- What are the costs and benefits of developing technical experts versus developing intermediate technical experts with an enhanced information management/research capability?

- How does teamwork affect technical performance? What do we mean by "teamwork?" Is it an appropriate concept for technical performance?

THE POTENTIAL CONTRIBUTIONS OF RESEARCH

As described above, there are many interesting, relevant questions and issues confronting tax practitioners and practice leaders. On a daily basis, these issues are being discussed in small and large groups. They are being studied by task forces. Outside management consulting firms are being called in to offer guidance. Positions of competitors are being examined. Debates are raging. With or without the contributions of researchers, decisions on these issues are being made and will continue to be made because they must be made in order to carry on business. How can researchers contribute?

First, researchers can propose research projects that address the needs of tax practitioners. Although researchers should design studies that represent the cutting-edge of research methods and contribute to the advancement of behavioral tax research, choices for new research studies and long-term research programs must be equally driven by a goal of producing results that are relevant and meaningful to practice. Thus, at some point during the development phase of a new research project, the researcher should engage in a dialogue with practitioners. If the researcher is successful in communicating how the expected results will contribute to practice, i.e., by addressing one of the questions described above or other questions or modifications suggested by the practitioners, then the researcher will find an eager and receptive audience for the proposal and may be able to secure funding and/or cooperation for the research. The researcher can also be confident that, upon completion, the research effort will be well received by the practice community.

Second, researchers can contribute by bringing greater rigor and validity to the study of questions and issues that practitioners are facing. Often, practitioners are forced to make decisions based on the best information available, but with less information than they would like to have. The application of research methods to these practice problems can provide that missing information and improve the validity of available information that is used by practice managers to make strategic decisions for the policies and strategies to sustain and grow the practice.

For example, suppose a firm's practice management committee is selecting an electronic tax software/database for tax compliance and/or research. Further suppose the committee is composed of a small number of tax partners and that this decision is to be made after receiving bids from several suppliers. These partners also may ask for input from the firm's computer network specialists. However, it would be highly unusual for the decision makers to have the benefit of a carefully designed experiment or research study that can answer the following questions: How do the differences in features among the available products (e.g., user interfaces, manuals, on-screen help, interfaces with existing firm software and hardware, reliability, flexibility, etc.) affect the target users' (e.g., first or second year staff) performance on representative compliance/research work assignments? What is the learning curve among users who are representative of the intended users? What are the types and frequencies of complaints/praises for the various products from the representative users? Without conducting some research, whether by survey, field study, or controlled experiment, critical information about the various products may never enter the decision making process. This information may surface, however, in the middle of busy season when it becomes apparent that tax staff are working 20 percent longer to perform tasks due to some inefficiency or deficiency of the newly installed system.

Few tax practice problems exist that cannot benefit to some degree by the contributions of research. Why, then, are practitioners so skeptical of the contributions of academic researchers? Three reasons are: (1) the scope of published academic research in accounting is so broad that very little of it is relevant to practitioners' immediate concerns with meeting the expectations of clients and employers for technical and business consulting work products; (2) the nature of published academic research contains methodological discussions that are incomprehensible to non-Ph.D.s; and (3) behavioral tax researchers have not yet addressed many questions and issues that are relevant to tax practitioners. Does this mean that academic researchers have no contribution to make? No, it simply means that there are many research opportunities that have not yet been explored and developed. Some of these have already been suggested in this chapter. Others may be discovered or ascertained by discussions with experienced tax professionals.

Once a research question that is relevant to tax practice has been identified, the next issue for the behavioral tax researcher is to identify an appropriate research methodology. The full range of social science research methods and tools should be considered, including in-person, mail and telephone surveys; field studies; quasi-experiments; controlled experiments; and archival studies. Because behavioral tax research has existed as a field of research for less than ten years, there is a particular need for descriptive and theory building research. Qualitative research such as in-person interviews and focus groups should not be overlooked in a rush to design and complete quantitative studies that may conform more closely to the expectations of journal reviewers but overlook or omit critical environmental and contextual features of tax practice.

Surveys are particularly appropriate for developing descriptions of the nature of, and current responses to, practice problems in all three areas of business/tax consulting, practice management, and technical expertise. Because of the paucity of research on tax practice issues, descriptive research is very important to further identify researchable issues, to describe relevant environmental criteria, and to develop theories for explaining and predicting behavioral responses to changes in practice conditions.

Field studies that develop and illustrate or test hypotheses about practice behaviors would be particularly useful. Some examples include the nature of individual compliance and research activities, communications and interactions between tax professionals, communications and interactions between tax professionals and clients, and communications and interactions between tax professionals and IRS agents.

Quasi-experiments and controlled experiments that describe and test theories about individual and group performance on solving business/tax, practice management, and technical problems are needed. In particular, research directed at improving performance on any of these dimensions would be very useful.

Archival studies using working papers of actual engagements are also potentially beneficial for describing current practice behaviors, establishing standards, and developing benchmark performance levels. Such archival studies would be very useful for guiding the development of experimental materials for quasi-experiments and controlled experiments.

CONSTRAINTS AND HOW TO OVERCOME THEM

Several constraints or obstacles threaten the potential of behavioral tax research for moving forward, contributing to the profession of business/tax accounting, and developing as an academic discipline and research field. These obstacles include:

- Poor opinion of research by practitioners
- Limited access and funding
- Low emphasis on relevance as a criterion for academic publications
- Lack of a community or "users' group" of behavioral tax researchers.

The first three items in this list are interrelated to some degree. As discussed in the prior section, many practitioners have a poor opinion of research conducted by academics because they see little relevance in it. This poor opinion, in turn, can be a barrier to researchers' access to tax accountants for (1) open-minded discussion of the potential benefits of research, (2) specific discussions and input for identifying research projects, (3) participation in the development, administration, and interpretation of research studies, and (4) funding for time, data collection, travel, and assistance for research.

Acceptance of research by practitioners will continue to be an uphill battle for behavioral tax researchers as long as the overwhelming volume of published academic research in accounting has little relevance to tax practice. Since behavioral tax research is likely to continue to be a relatively minor percentage of published research, behavioral tax researchers should be prepared to proselytize whenever the occasion presents itself. Researchers should be prepared to explain to tax professionals the goals, methods, and potential contributions of behavioral tax research, and then to back their statements up with examples of relevant research proposals, designs, and results.

At least four avenues are open for researchers to gain access for conducting behavioral tax research. Research grant programs such as the Ernst & Young Tax Grant Program and the Price Waterhouse Tax Fellowship program actively solicit research proposals and are currently providing both funding and access to tax professionals for behavioral tax research projects. Also, the National Science Foundation and numerous private foundations solicit research proposals for which behavioral tax research is eligible. In addition to formal grant programs, many public accounting firms support private foundations that offer funding and support to accounting education. Although these foundations do not regularly solicit proposals, many of these foundations regularly receive and consider proposals for which behavioral tax research certainly would be eligible. A third avenue is direct contact with a tax accountant in a local practice office of a large firm. This contact could be a practitioner with whom the researcher has a personal relationship or a firm's tax practice manager or recruiting or human resources director. A fourth avenue is direct contact with tax accountants in small firms. When the goals of the particular research study can be met by participants with small firm backgrounds, access usually is easier because these tax accountants receive fewer requests for participation than do tax accountants in large firms.

We have noted that one barrier to the future success of behavioral tax research is the perceived lack of relevance of published academic research to practice problems and issues. We also have suggested that, given the relatively early stage of behavioral tax research, there is a need for descriptive and theory building research. To the extent that these suggestions go unattended because researchers perceive such approaches to be unpublishable, an additional barrier exists in the form of current publication standards emphasizing experimental control and theory testing as opposed to exploratory and descriptive research and research methods such as field studies and surveys for which experimenter control is not high. Similarly, a barrier exists to the extent that behavioral tax research is not considered "accounting" research, and therefore is not eligible for publication in the journals in which accounting researchers are expected to publish by tenure and promotion committees, university administrators, and peers at other institutions.

Because behavioral tax research is an emerging area of accounting research, behavioral tax researchers also, unfortunately, face resistance from other (nontax) accounting researchers. Researchers should be prepared to explain and defend their choices of research topics and methods to nontax accounting researchers and to journal editors and reviewers. Researchers also should be prepared to explain the motivation for research studies in terms of the business and accounting issues, behaviors, and implications as well as those specific only to tax. Similarly, researchers should rigorously explain, document, and defend the validity of the research methodologies selected and employed, whether qualitative or quantitative and regardless of the degree of control employed. In addition, researchers should refer to the use of the research methods in other behavioral disciplines to help establish the validity of those methods for behavioral tax research.

Academic researchers, probably by nature, tend toward independence which is both positive and valuable in fostering creativity in research direction and design. However, successful development of the field of behavioral tax research, as well as the pace of development, would be greatly assisted by the creation of a community of scholars. The potential research domain for behavioral tax research, i.e., the breadth and number of issues that are relevant to tax practice, as well as the swirling currents of the present sea change for which research results would be timely indeed, suggest that the collective research agenda could be accelerated to the extent researchers interested in this area can agree on the directions for future research, including, for example:

- Parsing research topics into discrete projects.
- Establishing priorities for discrete projects.
- Setting guidelines for appropriate participant-task matching.
- Developing valid instruments for measuring knowledge, skills, and performance.
- Commenting on research design prior to implementation.
- Encouraging replication and extensions of research to establish both internal and external validity.

Such a community of behavioral tax researchers could assist each other and serve as a liaison between the Academy and Practice to bring focus to the conjunction of researchable issues that are relevant to Practice and to bring the relevance of research to the attention of Practice. Without such a community of scholars—whether organized formally or informally—behavioral tax research is likely to follow a meandering path similar to that of behavioral research in other accounting subdisciplines in which certain issues and methods become "research fads" for a while, until replaced by the next faddish issue or method.

Now What?

We are at the dawning of a new, urgently needed, exciting, potential partnership between accounting Practice and the Academy. This partnership is new because the field of behavioral tax research is new; it is urgently needed because of the structural changes that are occurring in the tax accounting profession. These structural changes provide a window of opportunity for collaboration and synergy between researchers and practitioners that has not been present before. Changes affecting Practice require a prompt response by practitioners. Researchers can provide valid information to decision makers within the practice community.

This partnership is also exciting because it offers an opportunity to academic researchers to bring their skills and talents to bear on practical problems that have real-world consequences, i.e., to see the immediate impact of their research on how people work. In addition, it is exciting because it offers the prospect of better information for practice decision-makers—information that should, in turn, produce better decisions.

Accounting Practice and the Academy do not share a successful history of collaboration or partnership on research, however. The potential exists for accomplishing the mutual goals, but practitioners and researchers must be willing to explore and understand the potential contributions of practice and research for the advancement of each field, and individuals must be willing to exercise good faith, combined with good business judgment, for this potential partnership to succeed. The path that lies ahead for collaboration between practitioners and behavioral tax researchers may prove to be smooth or rocky, but the journey is one that should be taken.

SUMMARY

In this chapter, we have identified many practical, researchable issues relevant to tax practice. The overall theme for Practice today is change—change that is having a substantial impact on firms and individual tax accountants. We have examined these issues through three facets: the tax accountant as business adviser, practice manager, and technical expert. For each facet, we have described the background of practice and suggested researchable issues.

Behavioral tax researchers have great potential for providing valid information to improve the quality of decision making and action for many of the issues currently facing practice managers and individual tax accountants. The rapid development of collaborative strategies for practical research projects that focus on issues relevant to Practice and that are designed with the rigor demanded of quality academic research will lead to immediate improvements in the capabilities of professional firms to meet and exceed the needs of their clients and of their own tax professionals. In most commercial endeavors, businesses that place a high priority on research and development, and demonstrate that priority through the commitment of resources, will gain competitive advantages over the long-run. Since the primary asset and product of professional tax firms is the creative expertise of their professionals, it is merely a matter of good business strategy to invest in research and development to continually seek new and improved methods for developing the firm's internal resources for producing expert tax advise and consulting for the external market. Behavioral tax research can supply that needed R&D for professional tax firms.

AUTHOR INDEX

INDEX

155